TABLE OF CONTENTS

INTRODUCTION

WHAT IS SELF-ESTEEM AND WHY IT IS IMPORTANT.

Self-esteem what is it, and how important is it?

What is self-esteem?

Self- esteem is having a positive attitude towards yourself. Therefore, self-esteem basically implies loving and respecting yourself.

Not everyone has the same self-esteem. We can see people who underestimate themselves to the point of not loving themselves as they are; or others to whom the opposite happens.

Why is it important to develop our self-esteem?

It is very important to develop, work, and improve our self-esteem daily. Self-esteem helps us feel much better about ourselves, which influences our behavior. Therefore, good self-esteem can help us to:

Getting to love ourselves as we are. Be good to ourselves. Confident and above all, being in tune with yourself.

When we know each other perfectly, we know what our strengths and weaknesses are. Therefore, this allows us to work on our virtues to the point of developing the best we have of ourselves, thus achieving self-realization as people.

Furthermore, when we face the world with a totally positive vision, we are much more capable of achieving our goals and objectives. Many times what psychologists call: "The prophecy of self-fulfillment " happens. For example, if you think that you are not going to be able to achieve something, surely you are not going to achieve it (because you are not going to do many of the things that you would have to do to be able to achieve it); otherwise, with a much more positive and proactive vision, we can achieve everything we set out to do.

When you are good with yourself, you will be reflected in your behavior and relationship with the environment. Therefore, a person with good self-esteem will be able to interact much better with new people, interact much more positively, establish more lasting relationships, etc.

What is necessary to develop self-esteem?

Self-knowledge: the first and most essential step to develop our self-esteem is self-knowledge. Self-knowledge, or self- awareness, means knowing yourself. It is about knowing how each of us is, knowing ourselves deeply. Know our strengths and weaknesses, our strengths, and our weaknesses.

Self-acceptance: as a second step, it is essential to accept ourselves as we are. It is very important to accept yourself unconditionally.

Empower ourselves: on the other hand, it is very important to be aware of our potential. Once we have met and accepted, we will be aware of our strengths. We must empower and develop them to make the most of ourselves.

Minimize weak points: it is very important to work on our weak points. We must work them without obfuscating ourselves. We know that they are our "Achilles heel," and that is why we will work with them more calmly and delicately. But we will never push them away and forget them.

Conduct ourselves positively: and lastly, it is very important to conduct ourselves positively. In other words, consider ourselves in a positive way, in which we treat ourselves with respect and value ourselves positively. It is important to love and appreciate ourselves.

Can high self-esteem be negative?

It is very important not to confuse self-esteem with what psychologists call the Grandiosity Self-Assessment. The grandiose self-evaluation would be a positive distorted vision of oneself, that is, to see oneself much better than one really is. In this case, we could speak, for example, of narcissistic people. They would also enter into this distortion: delusions of grandeur or bipolar people in a manic state. In the latter case, they are people who believe they are capable of everything and are unstoppable, so they can pose a great danger to themselves.

A self - esteem too, can become negative if the person is not aware of it. However, it can also be an adaptive mechanism. Examples of these would be: high confidence to achieve our goals, high motivation for certain jobs, self-fulfillment prophecy, maintaining hope...

Self-esteem is a critical and positive self-evaluation of oneself. Furthermore, true self-esteem is total and unconditional. It is very important to work and improve it in order to achieve our goals, have a positive vision of our environment, and live happier with ourselves and with others.

PART 1

CHAPTER - 1
WHAT IS HEALTHY SELF-ESTEEM?

Self-esteem is a simple word. It is the merit and value that we apply to ourselves.

By maintaining our self-esteem, we will value ourselves as worthy people in the world. If the esteem is low, our life will be dull and gray. And if we maintain high self-esteem, this could be the key to happiness in our life.

Healthy Self-Esteem

Your own self-esteem, however, is somewhat more fundamental than the normal "highs and lows" associated with changing situations. For people with healthy self-esteem, normal daily ups and downs can lead to temporary fluctuations in how they feel about themselves, but only momentarily. On the contrary, for people with low self-esteem, these "ups and downs" can cause them a lot of suffering.

Healthy self-esteem centers on our ability to accurately evaluate ourselves (know ourselves) and to be able to accept and value ourselves unconditionally. This means being able to really recognize our strengths and limitations (which are part of being human) and, at the same time, accept ourselves as worthy and valuable without conditions or reservations.

When we were little, our successes (and failures) and the way they were treated by members of our closest family (father, mother, grandparents ...), by our teachers, coaches, religious authorities, and by our colleagues, all contributed to the creation of our basic self-esteem.

An adult who has healthy self-esteem was given this gift in childhood. This could have been done in many ways. Probably one of the most important is that he was praised for his accomplishments. Children were spoken to with respect and listened to, thus contributing to their healthy self-esteem in adulthood. These children were hugged often and given the necessary attention, experiencing some kind of success in their school or sports activities.

On the other side, we have to identify childhood for those adults who have low self-esteem. These children were often harshly criticized, yelled at or hit, and little attention was given to them in the nearby environment to which they belonged. Perhaps they were ridiculed and even teased as they experienced failures in their young lives. They were made to feel that they had to be perfect to be valued, and the failure associated with particular situations was interpreted as a failure of their entire being.

It's sad, isn't it? Think of a child treated that way. What

is even sadder is the effect this treatment has on their lives as adults. We are shaped and shaped by our experiences.

SOME OF THE CHARACTERISTICS OF HEALTHY SELF-ESTEEM ARE:

Live consciously. Learn to live more consciously every day. Do this by listening to myself. I watch my reactions. I listen to my body and ask myself: "Am I hungry now, or am I only eating because it is time to eat?

Take care of your body, your mind, spirit, and emotions. I take care of my body, doing gymnastics, eating healthy. Emotionally, releasing my negative emotions. Mentally: reading and learning new things. Spiritually: meditating, praying, or being silent.

Learn from our own mistakes. Learn to say: "I made a mistake" and learn from the mistake. We all make mistakes, and the best way to understand is by learning from them.

Listen to the opinion of others. Why don't we listen to others? Because many times we want to be right. For a long time, I was like that, always wanting to be right.

Respect the differences of others. We are all different.

Respecting the differences of others does not mean that we will agree with them, but that we understand that they have the right to be different.

Take responsibility for your own life. I grew up in an environment where self-responsibility did not exist. It was always the other's fault or something external to blame. When I started taking responsibility for my life, my life began to change.

To be able to speak and act from our own convictions. I was always afraid to speak my truth because I was raised to be a "good baby" and to please others. Over the years, I have learned to speak my truth, and this has made me feel very good because I have maintained loyalty to myself.

THE IMPORTANCE OF BUILDING A HEALTHY SELF-ESTEEM

In psychology, "self-esteem" is defined as the way we value ourselves. Some people have very high self-esteem, and others quite low.

It does not have to do with boasting, but rather just appreciating and valuing those achievements that we achieve, for which there is no need to vilify anyone or to belittle our own work. In fact, self-esteem is important because it has an impact on life and decisions, and, on the other side, it is one of the bases of our mental health.

A person with healthy self-esteem has the confidence to seek what he wants without making another person feel unworthy.

But the good news is that while we can consider our self-esteem to be originally forged in our first years of life, we can also rebuild it. And the possibilities to do it, we have all. It has to do with building something different.

To start this process of rebuilding self-esteem, three things must be changed:

- the attitude with which things are approached,

- expectations about it, and

- the way of thinking and interpreting events that occur.

"They are all variables that we can act on because they are possibilities that are within us." The lawyer clarifies us.

PRACTICAL RECOMMENDATIONS FOR US TO APPLY IN OUR DAILY LIVES AND WE CAN BETTER HEAL OR CONTROL OUR SELF-ESTEEM AND DEPART FROM THERE, VARIOUS FIELDS OF MENTAL HEALTH AND LIFE:

Focus on the present. If we eagerly turn to the future, we will not be able to create the tools to reach that intended good destiny. Being located in the present helps to improve self-observation to get to know us better and to make better contact with our resources and powers and also with our weak points (to improve them). If you focus better on the present moment, you will calm down and have a broader view.

- Homework: 15 minutes of meditation per day, exercised with perseverance, will greatly contribute to your being more located in the present.

Exercise being aware of what you are thinking (your thoughts are just thoughts and not facts) and how you are feeling it. According to how you think, it is how you construct your reality, and consequently, how you conceptualize life will influence how you communicate with others, what actions (and reactions) you will have. Being in touch with your thoughts will allow you to construct your realities as more positive (and enabling) or more negative (and limiting). Being aware of this internal dialogue will allow us to detect the negative tendency, stop it and let the thought go (let go), not taking it as absolute truth, but as a possibility only.

- Task: this work of focusing on thoughts, recognizing them, letting go of some, is something that is exercised (mindfulness technique).

- Dedramatize: do not fear thoughts. They are just simple ideas unless we translate their influence into reality by turning them into facts. Look at them in context, relativize the dreaded influence.

- Task: incorporate humor so as not to fall into catastrophic thoughts.

- Practice gratitude: to be grateful, it is necessary to be able to see how positive life is and that each one of us has.

- Task: write in a notebook every day, ten positive or beautiful things that we saw, did, or happened to us.

Be aware of the accompaniment your body does to emotions. It is incongruous to adopt a defeated or tired body attitude and feel activated and ready to feel stronger and more positive.

- Task: Stand up straight, relax your shoulders, lift your chin, and relax your open arms at the side of your body. You will create an optimistic body attitude that will end up influencing your way of moving in the world.

- Seek to be positive: The negative things you hear or see will influence your mood. It is not about being uninformed or denying things, but incorporating a more positive and enabling vision (without losing realism).

- Task: provide positive stimuli (listen to music or watch videos with positive messages, look for positive news that occurs in our reality and in the world), and thus counteract the balance regarding negative thoughts that may be influencing us.

- Surround yourself with positive people: it is very difficult to have a positive perspective of life, of yourself and of the things that happen if you constantly receive a negative attitude about it, from the people around you.

- Task: Get together with people with energy and desire to do things that are physically and mentally healthy, that find enjoyment in the things of their life.

- Be supportive: kindness towards others enriches us, and fills us with a feeling of joy, connects us with the best of ourselves.

- Task: every day, try to have at least one act of kindness towards others, whoever they are.

Lose the fear of criticism. Fear of criticism can prevent you from doing what you really want to do. It works as a mental barrier. There are two types: personal, which helps to apply humor and relativize the comment and ultimately ask for a change in behavior. And those that refer to any task you are doing. Ask for specifications in this regard and take them as a learning opportunity.

- Task: practice to tolerate criticism, starting with those that are from people who are further from your affections (these are the most difficult not to be influenced).

- Focus on the possibilities: among so many things that you cannot do and so many that you can do, focus on the latter. Instead of wasting time and energy on things you can't do, spend time thinking about how you are going to do something you can do.

- Task: Look at the little things at the possibilities instead of the barriers. For this, exercise your psychological flexibility. And when you see the little positive things, congratulate yourself because they will contribute to enriching your personal universe.

Accept the moments of sadness. Sometimes, inevitably, you will feel sad. In these cases, it is better to accept them, see them as something normal in life, and calm down, realizing that they are temporary. It will happen.

Task: before a negative event, do not despair. It will happen. And again, the sun will rise.

10 CHARACTERISTICS OF A PERSON WITH A HEALTHY AND BALANCED SELF-ESTEEM

Take a pencil and paper and take aim; you will surely be surprised and discover things that you already do:

- YOU TRUST YOURSELF, allowing you to MAKE DECISIONS more easily, regardless of whether they are correct or not.

- You dare TO ASSUME RISKS and accept the RESPONSIBILITIES derived from all your actions.

- You know how to EXPRESS CRITICISMS properly, without attacking, and YOU ACCEPT YOUR MISTAKES.

- The problems do not scare you, you face them and also looking SOLUTIONS.

- You know your LIMITS, so you demand the right thing.

- You ACCEPT yourself as you are, with your VIRTUES and your DEFECTS.

- You know how to say NO to others WITHOUT experiencing guilt.

- You feel AUTONOMOUS and INDEPENDENT with respect to what others think, say, or do.

THE BENEFITS OF HEALTHY SELF-ESTEEM

You accept changes better, and the ability to assume them, you are better prepared to face problems both personally and at work or professionally developing resilience, the ability to resist and overcome adversities in life.

You feel more secure, and you respect yourself. You have a good opinion of yourself with more confidence and responsibility.

- More creativity, flexibility, realism, assertiveness, optimism, and good humor.

- You accept your own personality, affirm your needs, and make mistakes. You reaffirm your values, you know yourself more, and you feel loved.

- More quality in your affective relationships and better and effective communication. You build more open and sincere relationships based on respect and justice. The sense of belonging to the group is awakened.

- More successes than failures. You know your strengths, you enjoy the effort to achieve an achievement more, and you persist and persevere.

- There is a close relationship between healthy self-esteem and our ability to achieve what we set out to do. Your actions feedback on your self-esteem. Your level of self-esteem increases or decreases with your actions.

CHAPTER - 2

WHAT SELF-ESTEEM IS NOT

Self-esteem, that concept so widely used by everyone.... Do we really know what it is? It is something so little palpable and at the same time, it seems that we all know whether or not we have self-esteem. We know that it is not static, but that it is a fragile and changing process that increases when we live respecting our own values and decreases every time we behave away from our values.

NOT SELF-ESTEEM

Having a good self-concept is not always good, not every moment.

Nor is it being successful, because success itself does not guarantee good self-esteem.

Having self-love does not justify that we can harm others.

Having acceptance of oneself does not guarantee to save oneself from the crises or the low moments.

It is not feeling superior to others, nor above them.

Where do we build our SELF-ESTEEM?

Throughout childhood, our sense of identity, belonging, as well as our perception of ourselves are being built, all through the interactions we establish with people who are meaningful to us.

It is built in contact with other people, mainly our parents. But also, through family, friends, teachers. Everyone in one way or another has an influence on our perception of ourselves. Also, when we become adults; the environment, acquires an important role that adds to the experiences during childhood, and to the successes and failures that we have had throughout life.

An environment with destructive messages, or simply little validators, allows us to acquire low self-esteem. Furthermore, if we are not consistent with our values and beliefs or find it difficult to live with parts of ourselves, all that influences and directly attacks our self-esteem.

IF IT IS SELF-ESTEEM

Self-esteem is the assessment that each one makes of himself. Self-esteem includes concepts such as: self-confidence, respect for oneself, responsibility understood as being responsible for one's life, being an active protagonist. In addition, self-esteem also encompasses all the beliefs we have about ourselves. All this is complemented by being consistent with our values.

Therefore self-esteem has to do with: Self-worth of ourselves and at the same time self-respect, which can be translated into:

- Accept ourselves as we are.

- Respect ourselves.

- Take good care of ourselves as best we can.

- Manage our emotions.

- Accept reality as it is.

- Trust in ourselves.

- Take responsibility for our own life and be active protagonists of it.

- Affirm ourselves in front of others.

- Be able to manage conflicts

- Give us permission to enjoy, to take care of ourselves

Reviewing those messages that have built our self-esteem over the years, in addition to reviewing our perceptions, emotions, and relationships with ourselves and also with others are the first steps to increase our self-esteem.

In the universe, there is no other person exactly like you. I am me, and everything I am is unique, I am responsible for myself, I have everything I need here and now to live fully. I can choose to manifest the best of myself, I can choose to love, be competent to find a meaning in life and an order to the universe, I can choose to develop, grow and live in harmony with myself, with the rest of the people. I am worthy to be accepted and loved exactly as I am, here and now. I love and accept myself; I decide to live fully from today".

CHAPTER - 3
COPING: WHAT NOT TO DO

We tend to value everything that we can do at this time in our lives, but we do not take into account what we are missing. As self-esteem conditions our life and our actions, certain things will depend on whether it is high or low. In this way, there will be several things that we can miss by not having self-esteem at its optimum.

What i lose

Self-confidence is the first step to be able to live a full experience. It generates vital situations that fill us and satisfy us, we dare and we go to greater achievements. So what happens when we have low self-esteem? That there are numerous things that we will be ceasing to live, we will not be achieving or we will not be doing.

Low self-esteem negatively conditions our lives, both on a daily basis and in great achievements or events. In fact, there are six things that we will be unable to do without valuing and respecting ourselves:

1. Take care of my image

When I do not consider myself or do not value myself, I do not consider it important to take care of my image. The clothes I wear, the sport I do or the food I choose at the supermarket are usually not the most correct. We move by inertia and make decisions that harm us, both inside and outside. That neglected image that we have internalized, we also project it outwards.

2. Make decisions

Since I am not sure of myself, I don't usually make decisions. This happens because either I do not value almost anything, or I think that my opinion is not important and I am going to be wrong. In this way, it is the others who choose for me, I lose control of my life and I do not know where I am going.

3. Celebrate

If good things appear in someone's life, it is normal to enjoy it, especially when it is an achievement. People with low self-esteem do not do it, believe that they do not deserve it or that what they have achieved is not the product of their effort. They are not taken into account when doing it or when enjoying the arrival at the finish line.

4. Review

As my opinion is not important, I do not give it. I do not express my needs, I do not speak about what I like or I do not contradict you when you are wrong. I do not own my words and I do not express them. It is one of the big mistakes we make when we have low self-esteem.

5. *Healthy relationships*

Since my self-esteem is not healthy, neither are my relationships. In fact, I usually surround myself with people who take my energy or take advantage of me. I can easily fall into toxic relationships.

6. *Live*

If I rely on everything my low self-esteem won't let me do, I realize that I'm not really living, I'm just going through life. I am not aware of the days nor process what is happening. Everything is always the same.

Low self-esteem is part of the biggest problems that a person can have, since it negatively influences practically all areas of their life. They have bad relationships, do not express their needs and are influenced by the rest. Control of life has been lost, although everything is reversible and can always be recovered.

CHAPTER - 4

FACING DOUBT, FEAR

AND THE UNCERTAINTIES

OF CHANGE

Anticipatory anxiety. Have everything under control

If you wonder what anticipatory anxiety means, perhaps the most illustrative thing is to suggest that you think about those predictions that you and we all sometimes make about what will happen with some future event that affects us. This in principle is normal; we all make evaluations of the events and the decisions that we are going to make. But if the way to deal with this situation is to put ourselves in the worst of the outcomes by emitting a catastrophic prophecy, which consequently generates excessive worry and anguish and obsessive thinking, focused exclusively on the worst predictions, we would be talking about anticipatory anxiety, which It can be expressed according to the intensity with different symptoms, even in the form of panic attacks.

The problem is always the emotions that accompany the state of insecurity for the future: anxiety, fear, irritability, sadness or anger. They are all caused by our "futures".

All of them have to do with our resilience or the ability to face adversity, our tolerance for a negative event to happen. In fact, this low tolerance is so frequent that for many and many the saying: "Better known bad than good to know" has become a way of leading their lives.

There are people who, due to their personality traits, want to have everything under control , cannot bear improvisation or ignore any detail of what is going to happen, they need to have everything planned, structured... and this is almost never possible, we should all know: life is not it is usually predictable.

The inadequate handling of the fear of what will happen, that fear of what the future holds for us can condition us in many areas of our lives, specifically in a very important one, to make decisions. Decision-making on issues such as a possible separation, changing jobs, changing houses, and changing schools for children... can become unrealistic feats if we seek absolute certainty, that perfect decision, without a trace of error, of defect.

We mustn't just forget that life is a constant change, and decisions are necessary. Many times our anticipations lead us not to take them and if we avoid them we will not advance and we will remain stagnant, without giving us the opportunity, above all to learn, to explore, and consequently to be able to improve the following decisions and of course we will continue to focus on fear as a way of handling the unknown, uncertainty.

Making decisions and making mistakes is always better

than not making any decisions.

But let's try to better understand how emotions work in decision making.

HOW BLOCKAGES WORK IN THE DECISION-MAKING PROCESS

Our emotional states have a direct relationship with our way of thinking, of interpreting situations; they are very determined by our internal dialogue. In this sense, uncertainty, fear of the future, are closely related to anticipations, with acquaintances. What if...? What if I get fired? What if he is unfaithful to me? What if the treatments don't work? What if my marriage doesn't work?... What if, what if...

On many occasions the concern we use it as a strategy to reduce our anxiety, we have become accustomed to giving many turns to a decision, not so much as a tool to decide the best option, but to stay in that state where we do not make any decision. We believe that it is better not to rush, we even tell ourselves that it is a very complex and difficult decision and that we have to dedicate time, but let's not fool ourselves, if we don't make decisions, not only are we not going to feel better, but we are not going to move forward, we will not be able to verify if it is a good option and consider other alternatives, in short we will be blocked, stagnant. What do we wait to decide? Do we really believe that all the questions that arise are answered? Do we believe that there is a perfect, complete decision?

Do you know that there is a maladaptive or pathological

concern and an adaptive and useful one?

Living is constantly making decisions, I know that it is not a comfortable thing although I have to say that as in so many other questions about behavior and thinking, you train and it is becoming easier.

In Sartre's phrase Man is condemned to be free» I think that by the term "condemned" he wanted to express that this freedom implies something that we cannot avoid: decision making , perhaps that is why we like it so much that someone tells us what should we do.

Living life fully means, without a doubt, making decisions, getting some right and others wrong, but moving forward. There is no point in anchoring yourself in fear of the future; you have to carefully observe what is happening here and now: living in the present.

THE 3 PRESENTS YOU CAN LIVE IN

A well-known psychologist: Ramón Bayes points out that there are 3 present:

- Present - Past: Being in the present but thinking about past situations.

- Present - Future: Being in the present thinking about what is going to happen.

- Present - Present: Being here, now, in the present situation, focused on what we can do.

The fear of the future is clearly associated with what Bayes called present - Future. The really productive and healthy thing is to be in the Present - Present, which is ultimately what we have some control over, what we have some capacity for action or change. But what arises more frequently is to anticipate ourselves, it is these anticipatory thoughts, and even more, the anticipatory anxiety generated by this style that catches us and generates great discomfort.

"Time passes, friends, time passes and being aware of each moment we live, helps us to take possession of our freedom".

Let us stop feeling trapped by our thoughts and emotions and work daily to accept or curb them, take charge of our lives and feel free again.

I do not want to conclude this article without a brief guide of 5 highly recommended practices to face those periods of anguish, of fear of the future.

5 PRACTICAL EXERCISES TO COMBAT UNCERTAINTY

- Identify the emotion, do not try to fight it, observe it, normalize it, do not be angry to feel it.

- Identify where the uncertainty, anxiety, fear comes from.... Inquire what is going through your head and ask yourself where you are: in the present?, in the past?, in the future?

- Do not spend much time in your conversations on the subject that worries you so much. Set yourself a maximum time to talk about it, otherwise you run the risk that all your conversations revolve around the same topic, and consequently all your thoughts.

- In those moments of recurring thoughts of fear, of anxiety, change your gaze, change the subject of your thought and direct it towards you, but do it thinking about what you like, what you want, your vital pleasures, take time, take care of yourself, Find those moments for you.

- Practice flexibility and spontaneity, life is pure movement, challenge yourself and do small exercises of exposure, to break your need to control things:

Go to the cinema without knowing what movie you are going to see.

Leave the house in the morning and take a walk around your city and go deciding at all times what you want to do, do not go with schedules or planning.

Anticipatory anxiety. Have everything under control

If you wonder what anticipatory anxiety means, perhaps the most illustrative thing is to suggest that you think about those predictions that you and we all sometimes make about what will happen with some future event that affects us. This in principle is normal; we all make evaluations of the events and the decisions that we are going to make. But if the way to deal with this situation is to put ourselves in the worst of the outcomes by emitting a catastrophic prophecy, which consequently generates excessive worry and anguish and obsessive thinking, focused exclusively on the worst predictions, we would be talking about anticipatory anxiety, which It can be expressed according to the intensity with different symptoms, even in the form of panic attacks.

The problem is always the emotions that accompany the state of insecurity for the future: anxiety, fear, irritability, sadness or anger. They are all caused by our "futures". All of them have to do with our resilience or the ability to face adversity, our tolerance for a negative event to happen. In fact, this low tolerance is so frequent that for many and many the saying: "Better known bad than good to know" has become a way of leading their lives.

There are people who, due to their personality traits, want to have everything under control , cannot bear improvisation or ignore any detail of what is going to happen, they need to have everything planned, structured ... and this is almost never possible, we should all know: life is not it is usually predictable.

The inadequate handling of the fear of what will happen, that fear of what the future holds for us can condition us in many areas of our lives, specifically in a very important one, to make decisions. Decision-making on issues such as a possible separation, changing jobs, changing houses, and changing schools for children... can become unrealistic feats if we seek absolute certainty, that perfect decision, without a trace of error, of defect.

We mustn't forget that life is a constant change, and decisions are necessary. Many times our anticipations lead us not to take them and if we avoid them we will not advance and we will remain stagnant, without giving us the opportunity, above all to learn, to explore, and consequently to be able to improve the following decisions and of course we will continue to focus on fear as a way of handling the unknown, uncertainty.

CHAPTER - 5
YOU ARE ENOUGH

Imagine someone who does not dare give their opinion when they are in a group.

Imagine someone who is not moving towards his goals, who is not going for what he wants.

Imagine someone who lives in fear of disappointing others, not liking them.

WHAT DO THESE PEOPLE HAVE IN COMMON? I'M TELLING YOU: DON'T BELIEVE ENOUGH.

If I think that I am not enough, I will not dare to say what I think, because I will think that it is not correct.

If I think that I am not enough I will not move towards my goals, because I think that I am not enough to reach them.

If I think that I am not enough, I will be afraid that others will not approve of me, that they will not like me .

"I AM NOT ENOUGH" IS ONE OF THE MOST FREQUENT BELIEFS IN PEOPLE WITH LOW SELF-ESTEEM.

And I have already told you many times how our beliefs determine what we achieve in our lives. How what you believe in you creates your reality.

BECAUSE DEPENDING ON WHAT YOU THINK OF YOURSELF, THIS IS HOW YOU WILL FEEL AND HOW YOU WILL BEHAVE.

For example, if you think that you are not enough to get that promotion in your work or for a man who interests you to notice you, you will feel insecure, small, little thing.

How will you behave? You will get nervous, you will stay blocked, you will say something that does not touch or you will not say anything...

Thus, you will fail in what you wanted to achieve, and that will confirm your belief that you are not enough. With which you will feel insecure again, small, little thing... and the circle will continue to rotate in the same way. The whiting that bites its tail.

This is how what you believe about yourself, your potential and your abilities, determines the results you get in your life.

HOW BELIEVING THAT YOU ARE NOT ENOUGH AFFECTS YOUR LIFE

How does believing and feeling affect you, even if you don't even realize it, that it's not enough? How is that belief, deep and unconscious, reflected in your life and in what you achieve?

I am going to give you real examples of people who have done my Self-Esteem program, so that you yourself can realize if this belief also affects you.

If I don't believe myself enough I will think that what others do has to do with me, I will take it personally. Thus, if a person is less sympathetic than I expected, I will deduce that it is because he likes me or because something has bothered me. There I am connecting with my belief that I am not enough.

If I think that I am not enough to like and to be loved as I am, I will live in fear that they will reject me and stop loving me.

I will be envious that another person is all that I think I am not, because that person will connect me with my feeling that I am not enough.

When I am with other people I will compare myself a lot and feel inferior. I will think that they are better than me and I will look small next to them, because I am not enough.

Someone who believes that it is not enough will be afraid of not finding a partner and, from that fear; it will cost him much more to find her.

More examples...

If I think I'm not enough, I will depend on the approval and recognition of others to feel good. I will do whatsoever it takes to get it, because I have learned that I am not enough for myself and that what I am worth depends on the validation of others.

If I think I am not enough as a person, I will lose my dignity by begging someone who loves me. And the worse that person treats me the more I will think that the problem is in me, because of course, I am not enough. So even with someone who despises me and treats me badly, I will feel guilty. Because deep inside of me what I believe is that this person does not treat me well because I am not enough.

But will I get something? No, nothing. Because if I don't respect myself, the person in front of me won't respect me either. If I don't believe myself enough, others will perceive the same of me, because they can only see what I show them. What they see in me and how they treat me is always a reflection of what I believe in myself.

And if I have a partner, I will be one of those people who say "I as a couple give everything because I want the other to be at ease, to feel good, to be happy." But I will not be well because I will feel that I do not receive as much as I give.

Sure, because if I don't value myself the others won't value me either!

Because nobody can value you if you don't value

yourself.

And the others always come to show you something. If you value yourself, you will find people who value you. If you do not value yourself, you will find people who do not value you, so you can realize it!

It's funny how this need to like someone happens to us even with people we don't care about; we don't even like how they are.

We idealize someone, we think that person is worth more, and we strive to like and approve of us. When what I see in that person does not speak about him, but about me. That I don't value myself, that I don't feel enough.

More examples...

Someone who believes that it is not enough will crush himself a lot for being the way he is, with that ruthless inner critic that I often talk about. The one that informs you that you are not nice enough, funny, outgoing, brave ... that you are not X enough to be loved.

And I do not care what you put in the place of the X ...

I am too sensitive, I am weak, I have no character, I am bland, I am shy, I am fearful, I am slow, I am short of mind, I am too introverted... It should not be like that, I am not as I should be ... I mean, I am not enough.

And, as I said before, believing that I am not enough will also influence my behavior and the results I get in my life and in my relationships.

For example, suppose I join a mountain group because I want to meet people. But when the first plan comes, I back off. I am beginning to think that what am I going to go for, that I am going to see if I do not fit in, that I am still not comfortable, that it is still people who already know each other and what I paint there ... What is under all these excuses? Feeling that I am not enough.

The same as someone who avoids or postpones problems, instead of facing them. Since he doesn't think enough to solve it or to do it well, he prefers to look the other way. And this is how his belief conditions what he achieves: nothing.

EITHER YOU BEHAVE LIKE A VICTIM OR YOU INSIST ON BEING PERFECT

When someone does not feel enough, they often learn to camouflage that feeling with insane behaviors.

It may be that she does it from the victim, making herself tiny and letting opportunities pass. For example, since my opinion is invalid, since I don't know enough, I'd better shut up and say nothing.

Or if there is something I love to do, like painting, writing or composing songs, but I don't feel enough, I will never show my talent to someone.

Or I will not express what I really want and I will end up doing what others say , with the feeling that I let them decide for me . Because I am not enough.

It may also be that, instead of camouflaging my belief

that I am not enough from the victim, I do so by overcompensating. That is, so that no one realizes that I do not feel enough, I will do a lot, I will try hard and I will be very perfect (to appear and give an image to others).

So even though deep down inside I still feel like I'm not enough, at least no one will notice.

For example, if I feel bad, if I'm sad or something bothers me, I won't tell anyone. So that no one realizes that I feel this way, that this is hurting me, that I am vulnerable...

It will be hard for me not to be right and I will need to convince others that what I say is correct.

I will take criticism very badly and that someone does not agree with me, because that makes me connect with my feeling that I am not enough.

For example, if my partner teases me about something I was wrong about, I will be defensive.

And since I demand so much, so much, and I want to make it so perfect to compensate for my feeling that I am not enough; I will leave things for the last moment.

In other words, if I force myself to be perfect, it is also because deep down inside I feel that I am not enough as I am, and I need to do very well and receive the approval and recognition of others to feel enough.

HOW TO START BELIEVING THAT YOU ARE ALREADY ENOUGH

The only possible solution is to change what I think of myself.

As long as I continue to believe that I am not enough, I will continue without being authentic, without giving my best, without being the protagonist of my life, always seeking the approval of others, finding people who treat me badly , putting others ahead from my...

And I assure you that you can change, that you can stop believing that you are not enough and start believing and feeling that you are , that you are much more than enough, that you are perfect and wonderful just the way you are.

Like each of the women I work with, you can too. I tell you how:

1. Identify where that belief comes from. You weren't born believing you weren't enough. It is not in your essence, it is something learned.

You learned to believe that about yourself from some experiences and comments in your childhood and adolescence.

For example, a girl who gets angry about everything. If she does everything wrong, if she never does anything right, if she gets a 7 and they tell her that for the next one a 9, if she could always have done better, she will feel that it is not enough. If no matter how much she does nothing, she will conclude that she is not enough.

Just like a girl whose father or mother are never at home, do not spend time with her, and are not affectionate, you can also believe that she is not enough.

The same as a girl who is compared a lot with her siblings or with other boys. Look how studious, who looks at what list she is, who looks smart, who looks curious, how beautiful she is... And so many comparisons that we sometimes hear as children and that also lead us to believe that "I am not enough".

This is how what we live as children shapes our self-concept and can lead us to live, as adults, from " to see what I do so that you approve of me and feel enough for you."

When what others think affects us too much, it is usually because it connects us with a part of our child that did not receive the affection or approval that he needed. And so, as adults, when feeling rejected, it is as if that wound was opened with which we learned to believe that "I am not enough."

2. Make a difference what you feel from what you are.

I can feel that I am not enough, but that does not mean that it is. In essence I am. We all are, and much more than enough.

What we are, what we are worth, is in our essence. From there you are enough; you are already perfect and wonderful as you are.

So you can accept that you don't feel enough now, but

remind yourself that in essence you are, that you know that you ALREADY are enough.

3. Connect with your essence and repeat to yourself what you already are.

For example, I am much more than enough.

I am valuable and perfect just as I am (this phrase is a great example of acceptance, because it means that I do not need to change anything about me, that everything is fine as it is).

Remember that the other was what you learned, the lie that you told yourself as a result of the experiences you lived. Reveal yourself to her and remind yourself, over and over, that you are enough.

Enough already. I do not need to demonstrate anything or receive the approval of anyone to be, because I ALREADY am.

4. Think about how you can behave if you already believed and felt that you were enough.

How would you behave in this kind of situation if you connected with your essence and with which you are already enough?

What would you do if you believed and felt that you are perfect and wonderful just the way you are?

For example, if I think I am enough, I will feel safe and the next time I talk to this friend, I will tell her about me and how I am feeling (instead of leaving me for the end or not giving importance to what I feel, as I did). When I thought it wasn't enough).

Do you see how to put it into practice? Well, you can start behaving as if you already believed and felt enough. Because you really know that you are, that in essence you are. And, because the path is made on foot.

CHAPTER - 6
YOU CAN, YOU MUST FEEL BETTER

Not feeling so great today and want to feel better soon? With these strategies you can quickly gather yourself together again. Don't keep walking around with a bad feeling!

Sometimes you just feel a little less

You cannot always be the sun in the house. Sometimes you just feel less well. A bad night, hassle at work, no inspiration, dull weather and so on. These are things that can influence your day and your mood.

You may suddenly feel lifeless without knowing exactly why. It can be a combination of circumstances (a boring day at work, nothing nice in the prospect, tired, not moved enough in recent weeks, stressed, etc.) so that you cannot pinpoint the exact cause.

Whatever the causes, you can often feel better by taking action. Do not linger in your annoying mood, but gather yourself and start doing something positive! The following steps can assist in you get back into a positive mood.

1. Find out why you feel bad is there reasons why you are not feeling well? **Grab** a notepad and write down the various causes that seem to be in your way. You may be able to pinpoint a clear cause right away, but it can also be several seemingly silly things.

That annoying comment from a colleague, all the things you have to arrange for your birthday party next week, too much work and too little fun, a dip in a good friendship and so on.

Once you have written these things down you can immediately distance yourself from them. Because you see that the causes are not as bad as they seem in your head, you can immediately feel a lot better.

2. Accept that you can feel bad

Try not to fight too hard against your feelings, but accept that you are just not feeling well. That's not to say you can't or shouldn't try to improve your mood.

If you accept that you just do not feel optimal today, you will relax. It's okay to feel less. It is the way it is . If you feel like improving your mood then you can try that. If not then not. It is your own choice!

3. Take a moment of rest for yourself

Time for yourself can have a positive impact on your feelings. Many problems and issues in your life are related to other people. By taking time for yourself you can come to yourself.

Do something you enjoy. Do you like to meditate? Then meditate, and try to completely let go of the world around you.

4. Get moving

Because 'feeling uncomfortable' is mainly a psychological affair, it can be nice to get to work physically. Your body and your thoughts influence each other. You get physical complaints from mental stress. You can also feel better psychologically the other way around by getting moving.

Exercise for an hour. You can go for a run, go to the gym, dance in the living room, it doesn't matter. Make sure to increase your heart rate for at least half an hour, and preferably a little longer.

During exercise, your body produces substances that will make you happy. It's kind of a natural shot of happiness. However, you have to work for half an hour! Exercising makes you physically tired and relaxed. This gives you a satisfied feeling, and it also helps you sleep deeper and firmer.

5. Take care of your body

Retire to the bathroom for a comprehensive grooming ritual. By working with your body in a positive way you will feel better in your own skin. It helps you clear your head.

Most people feel great after a nice warm shower. Pull out your best shower gel, face mask, exfoliating gel and body lotion from the closet and give the body the care it deserves.

6. Plan less than usual

Boost your confidence by planning less than usual. Grab your to-do list for today, and try to halve the number of tasks on it. Do not write down more than you can do, but less.

You can feel better about yourself if you have done something useful. Do not set the bar too high, and reward yourself for what you have achieved. It is better to finish a task list with three relatively small tasks completely than to get a large task list only partially done.

Completing tasks gives you satisfaction. Your self-confidence will get a boost, which will immediately make you feel better. These small tasks may lead to other tasks being performed. Do not make too high demands on yourself if you don't feel well.

7. Agree on something nice

Have something fun in mind. Arrange to have a drink with a friend, or book a restaurant with your partner. Make a special recipe tonight, invite your parents to dinner, rent a movie or agree with yourself that you will read in a nice book.

By having fun things ahead, you give life more shine. It doesn't need to be expensive, it has to be fun. A bike ride through the polder can be wonderful, just like an overnight stay in Brussels.

8. Take a nap

Maybe you are just tired? Sleep deprivation has all kinds of effects on both your body and your mind. If you have had too little sleep, it is difficult to stay inspired, happy and sparkling.

See if you can take a nap, or go to bed on time today. A good night's sleep works wonders.

Do you not fall asleep while you are tired? Then you may be especially mentally tired, but physically rested. You can compensate for this by exercising more during the day. Stress can tire your mind without making you really sleepy. Make your body tired, and then you sleep a lot better!

PART 2

EXERCISE TO BUILD AND BOOST YOUR SELF-ESTEEM, GROW CONFIDENCE AND STAY POSITIVE

SELF-CONFIDENCE

It is important to cultivate the habit of trusting in yourself because it is this that allows us to act with authority and property at all times, it prevents us from walking in doubt and fearful of what may happen.

Trusting in ourselves allows us to face life with less fear and more decision.

If two people are proposed to perform the same task, all other factors being equal, the one with the most self-confidence will do better and faster.

This, from the simplest task to the most complex.

But why does it seem like a great challenge to trust yourself?

Even if you are very talented and you have great skills under pressure, if you do not have great Self-Confidence, you will not be able to perform at your best.

For example, if you work in sales, it is one thing to read

a book and learn and understand sales techniques, but quite another will be to challenge yourself to go out and sell and consistently apply those techniques facing the customer prospect face to face. Therefore, the greatest limitation will not be the lack of knowledge on the subject or the lack of expertise, but the limiting belief that you will not succeed in doing it well, and that everything will be a failure because you do not trust yourself.

You may think that Self-Confidence is a matter of having a successful track record.

And certainly, although this can increase your self-confidence, you don't need a long history of success to feel confident.

Trust is a feeling of certainty, an inner resource that you can use whenever you want.

HOW DOES HAVING A LOW/NEGATIVE SELF-CONTROL AFFECT AN INDIVIDUAL

In everyday life, it is normal that in some situations we show a certain degree of "impulsiveness". When faced with danger, we tend to respond without thinking, which is because the emotional part of our brain takes over. It is not a negative thing; on the contrary, it allows us to respond quickly enough by drawing on our arsenal of instinctive responses.

However, when there is a problem controlling emotions and behavior in different situations, we can refer to an impulse control disorder. These problems are characterized by the tendency to execute actions too quickly, thoughtlessly and / or irrationally and the inability to inhibit such actions once they have been launched.

The person with a self-control problem is unable to resist a temptation, urge, or desire. There is also a tendency to seek immediate gratification, at the expense of long-term goals; that is, that person does not think about the consequences of their actions beyond the present.

THE DISORDERS ASSOCIATED WITH IMPULSE CONTROL PROBLEMS

Under the category of self-control problems are different disorders:

- Intermittent explosive disorder. Episodes of lack of self-control occur, manifested by disproportionate outbursts of anger over provocation, tantrums, and / or verbal disputes. Immediately afterwards, the person regrets his actions or recriminates himself for having lost control.

- Kleptomania. It is the irresistible urge to steal objects, even if they are worthless. Theft is not premeditated; the person simply sees the object and feels the desire to take it.

- Pyromania. It is the urge to start fires for pleasure.

- Pathological gambling It is a recurring gambling behavior. The person experiences an uncontrollable urge to play and gamble, he cannot avoid it even if he knows that this behavior is causing him harm.

- Trichotillomania. It is the urge to pull your hair out. In some cases it is accompanied by trichophagia.

- Onychophagia. It is a compulsive habit that leads the person to bite and eat their nails.

- Dermatilomania. It is a compulsive urge to scratch, excoriate or pinch the skin, to the point of injury.

- Compulsive buying. It is the irresistible urge to buy, even if the person does not need those products.

- Nervous tics. It is a compulsive movement that is repeated frequently. It can be simple, like a blink, or it can be more complex movements involving different muscle groups.

- Tourette syndrome. This neurological disorder is characterized by the presence of repetitive movements that are beyond the voluntary control of the person. In some cases sounds are also emitted, such as clearing your throat or even words.

In addition to impulse control disorders, we find other problems where lack of self-control is very present, such as addictions or compulsive intake.

SYMPTOMS INDICATE THE EXISTENCE OF AN IMPULSE CONTROL PROBLEM

If you identify with some of these situations, it is likely that you have a self-control problem:

- You feel an increasing inner tension that causes you emotional distress and prompts you to practice certain behaviors, even though you know they are harmful.

- You cannot control your behavior, you keep repeating that pattern even though you are aware that it does not make sense or that it is harmful to you and / or those around you.

- You often experience feelings of guilt, shame, and remorse after succumbing to your impulses.

- You tend to act impulsively, without reflecting on the consequences of your decisions, attitudes and / or behaviors.

- You have a tendency to seek immediate gratification, knowing that such behavior may go against your future plans and interests.

CONSEQUENCES OF LACK OF CONTROL

Depending on the type of disorder, a number of complications can appear:

- Alcohol and other substance abuse.

- Depression, coupled with feelings of guilt.

- Stress and anxiety.

- Family conflicts and difficulties in interpersonal relationships.

- Self-injurious behaviors.

- Labor problems.

- Economic difficulties.

- Low self-esteem and poor self-worth.

- Problems with justice.

It is not uncommon for people with an impulse control disorder to meet the diagnostic criteria for another mental health condition. In some cases, an impulse control disorder may cause symptoms of another mental illness to appear. Some of the most common concurrent disorders are:

- Depressive disorders

- Bipolar disorder

- Anxiety disorders

- Behavioral disorders

- Antisocial personality disorder

- Post-traumatic stress disorder

- Negative defiant disorder

TREATMENT TO PROMOTE SELF-CONTROL

An important component of impulse control treatment is learning relaxation techniques and practicing mindfulness to help you deal with anxiety and a sense of urgency. Numerous studies have shown that practicing mindfulness improves self-control ability by improving executive brain function.

EVALUATING PERSONAL DEVELOPMENT USING SWOT ANALYSIS

Why use SWOT analysis for ourselves?

As we have seen, it is a tool that can help detect barriers and limitations, find new solutions, and decide on the course. And these are points that we may need at a personal level at some point. It is because we have run out of work and find it difficult to find a new one. It is because we are not happy with what we have, but we cannot think of what other jobs we could do. In other words, to improve our self-esteem.

When we feel stuck and do not see a solution or do not know what to decide, it is usually because we may not see all the possible options, or we do not believe we have the resources to face the situation. At these times, reminding ourselves of our strengths and reflecting on all of our opportunities may be just what we need. Consciously admitting our weaknesses can be the first step to accept them and work on some of them.

Even blackening the threats, we think we could give us clues. That is, ideas for facets to improve or threats that could become opportunities if we change our focus or improve some knowledge, ability, or aspect of ourselves.

The SWOT analysis focuses on the four elements that are part of its acronym:

S: strengths,

W: weaknesses,

O: opportunities,

T: threats

You can create a list of internal and external opposites side by side and ask participants these questions: What are the strengths and weaknesses of our group, community or initiative and what opportunities and threats are we facing?

Internal		External	
Strengths	Weaknesses	Opportunities	Risks

Or if a simpler structure can help you brainstorm, you can group positives and negatives to think more broadly about your organization and its external environment.

Positive	Negative
<ul><li>Strengths</li><li>Advantage</li><li>Resources</li><li>Opportunities</li><li>Possibilities</li></ul>	<ul><li>Weaknesses</li><li>Limitations</li><li>Restrictions</li><li>Threats</li><li>Challenges</li></ul>

The third option to structure your SWOT analysis may be appropriate for broad initiatives that require detailed planning or many alternatives. "The TOWS matrix" has been adapted from the text by Fred David: "Strategic Management"

	STRENGTH 1. 2. 3. 4.	WEAKNESSES 1. 2. 3. 4.
OPPORTUNITIES 1. 2. 3. 4.	Opportunities-Strengths (OF) Strategy Use strengths to take advantage of opportunities 1. 2.	Opportunities-Weaknesses (OD) Strategy Overcome weaknesses by taking advantage of opportunities 1. 2.
THREATS 1. 2. 3. 4.	Risk Strategy-Strengths (RF) Use strengths to avoid threats 1. 2.	Threats-Weaknesses (AD) Strategy Minimize weaknesses and avoid threats 1. 2.

David gives us an example from the Soup Company where he emphasizes financial goals, but he can also link the items within a SWOT chart of strategy development.

	STRENGTHS	WEAKNESSES
	• Increasing current benefit rate • Good mood of the employees • Market share increase	• Unresolved lawsuits or lawsuits • The capacity of the plant has dropped • Lack of strategic management systems
OPPORTUNITIES • Unification of the European West • Increased awareness of the importance, for health, of properly selecting meals • The demand for soups	Opportunity Strategy - Strengths (OF) • Acquire a food company in Europe. (F1, F3 and O1) • Development of new and healthy soups. (F2, O2)	Opportunities-Weaknesses (OD) Strategy • Development of new products in other lines. (D1, O2, O3)

increases annually		
THREATS • Decrease in the value of the dollar • Cans are not biodegradable	Risk Strategy-Strengths (AF) • Development of biodegradable containers for soups (F1, A2)	Threat-Weakness Strategy (AD) • Close European operations that are not generating profits (D3, A1)

This example also exemplifies how threats can be turned into opportunities (and vice versa). The limitation of non-biodegradable cans creates an opportunity for development and leadership in the production of biodegradable containers. There are different formats that we can use for a SWOT analysis, including a basic SWOT format that you can use a system analysis for, don't be surprised if your strengths and weaknesses don't precisely match your opportunities and threats.

CHAPTER - 1

SELF-ESTEEM SURVEY

This test helps you assess your self-esteem. It is a set of perceptions, thoughts, evaluations, feelings and trends of behavior directed towards ourselves, our way of being, the features of our body and our character. The importance of self-esteem is that it affects our way of being and the perception of our personal worth. Therefore, it affects our behavior and the way we relate to others.

You must answer all the questions. Answer intuitively as it is important that the answer is as honest as possible. If you do not find an option that fits your way of being, choose the most similar one.

This test only provides guidance and has no diagnostic value.

TEST START

When someone seeks you for a favor that you don't have time or desire to do...

- Despite everything I do, I don't know how to say

no.

- I make an excuse no matter how silly I don't have to do that favor.

- I tell you the truth, that I don't feel like it or I can't do what you ask.

Someone comes to interrupt you when you are working or doing something that you consider important, what do you do?

- I attend you, but I try to cut as soon as possible with education.

- I attend to him without showing any rush to leave.

- I don't want interruptions, so I try not to be seen and someone else says I'm very busy.

When you're in a group, do you have trouble making decisions?

- It depends on the trust I have with the people in the group, it costs me more or less.

- I usually have no trouble making decisions, wherever.

- Yes, I usually have a hard time making any decision when I'm in a group.

- I would change a lot of things to feel better and be more comfortable with people.

- It would be fine, but I don't think it would change anything essential in my life.

In a group of people who argue, who do you think is right?

- Normally I have the reason.

- Not all, just some. Generally, most give valid versions of reality.

- All people contribute valid points of view.

Your superior protests or scolds you quite loudly for a job of yours saying that it is poorly done...

- I listen carefully, trying to divert the conversation to constructive criticism and to learn from my mistakes.

- That you raise your voice is not justified in any case. You have no right to treat me like this, so I cannot hear what you are saying until your tone of voice drops.

- It bothers me that he scolds me and I have a bad time.

You are very concerned about the impression you make on others, whether you like them or not...

- Very much, I cannot bear that someone has considered me badly.

- Not always, only when I'm especially interested in the other person's friendship.

- What others think of me will not influence my way of being.

Do you ask, inquire and find out what people prefer

about you and what they don't?

- Yes, although I do have some disappointments.

- Yes, and I enjoy getting to know myself through others.

- I don't ask anything; just in case I find answers that I would have preferred not to hear.

Do you think you could achieve anything you set your mind to?

- Only a few things I think of are possible.

- I have a hard time getting what I want, I don't think I could.

- With work, luck and confidence, surely you will.

Are you convinced that your work has value?

- I am not convinced, but I do what I can because it has a value.

- No, rather I think that many times it has no value.

- I am convinced that it has a lot of value.

I consider myself a shy person...

- Depending on the environment in which I move, I can be more or less shy.

- It is not difficult for me to make friends or interact in any situation.

- I think I am an especially shy person.

How do you feel when someone new to you first discovers a defect you were hiding?

- This question presupposes that I hide my defects, in any case my answer is that I do not care and that I prefer that I know them as soon as possible.

- I feel very bad and from that moment my relationship with that person is no longer the same.

- I find it uncomfortable, but I try not to give it more importance.

Have you been hurt by what someone else told you?

- Yes, I have been hurt many times.

- There is nothing they can say that can hurt me.

- Yes, but only by words spoken by very dear people.

If you could change something about your character, what would you change?

- Nothing.

- I don't know, there are many things.

- Something.

When you've had a love failure, who did you think was the fault?

- Mine, normally.

- Of the other, normally.

- Each failure is different, sometimes one

sometimes another.

If you do a great job, isn't it such a great job if no one recognizes you?

- Indeed, if no one recognizes the value of my work, it is not so worth it.

- The value of any work is independent of the judgment of whoever it is.

- The value of my work is the only one that can judge it.

Do you feel like nobody loves you?

- It is not that I feel it, it is true that nobody loves me.

- Yes, sometimes I feel that nobody loves me.

- No, only sometimes do I feel that they don't understand me, but it's not the same.

- People that everyone loves are worth nothing, only the greats generate hatred and enemies.

- I never feel like this, the people around me appreciate me.

If repeatedly in work meetings or study groups your ideas are not taken into account...

- I think that it is not worth the effort because my ideas are not as good as I thought and I try to attend to the ideas of others, leaving from now on to offer more ideas.

- I consider it an unfavorable statistic, but I continue to contribute my ideas if I come up with an interesting one.

- I leave the group, since my ideas are not taken into account and I try to form another one in which I am the leader or go solo.

Where do you think your way of being takes you?

- Towards constant improvement.

- To disaster.

- To normality.

CHAPTER - 2

FIND FAITH IN YOURSELF

It is essential to have faith in yourself, both for you to do well in your university career and for professional success. If you feel that you don't have this quality yet, you'd better work on it.

Having self-confidence is essential when it comes to being successful in an endeavor as it helps to combat your anxieties about a new project. If you don't have faith in yourself, follow these five practical tips:

1. Trust that you have made good decisions based on reliable information. Before making a decision, make sure you've done a lot of research. Once you have done this, you must have the confidence to take the next step regardless of the opinion of others.

2. Stop worrying about fear of failure. Many times we experience a feeling of premature failure that has nothing to do with reality. For example, before taking an exam. Don't let fear of failure paralyze you . Think that learning from mistakes is always healthy.

3. During transition periods, keep priorities clear. Every new project needs perseverance and determination. As much as eventualities or unplanned things arise, you should not change your priorities. If you have set out to finish an academic career and a job opportunity arises, do not let it discourage you or blur your studies.

4. Getting what you want means giving up some things. Continuing in line with what was stated in the previous point, you must be clear that chasing a dream often means having to give up things we want. Don't be afraid to make decisive decisions if the moment warrants it.

5. Go ahead and have faith that you will arrive safely. The best recipe for having faith in yourself is to have confidence in the decisions we make and, also, to lean on the people who love us and surround us. Don't hesitate to ask for advice from the people who know you best when you feel cloudy on your way. They will be able to help you restore your self-confidence and give you the strength to keep going on all your projects.

CHAPTER - 3
NOTICING NEGATIVE SELF-TALK

Like most of our behaviors, our negative (and also positive) internal thoughts and dialogue are learned; something that differentiates us from other species, which are based more on instincts. Without neglecting the genetic predispositions with which we are born, the truth is that what determines our way of thinking; feeling and then behaving are lived experiences, our learning. Therefore, if we have learned to speak to each other in a certain way, as we will see later, we can also unlearn to do so, instead learning other forms of more positive and constructive internal dialogue.

These forms of learning are in turn influenced by various factors, which condition the fact that we speak ill of ourselves:

- Motivational factors (for example, anxious people tend to interpret more situations as threatening).

- Family and educational (for example, on many occasions, in our self-critical dialogue, an authoritarian father speaks, or a teacher who is not very reinforcing).

- Cultural (for example, our thoughts associated with judgments of reality are contextual, that is, reality is good or bad depending on the culture from which it comes).

- Friends and colleagues (for example, there are people who think and do autodialogues similar to those of their peer group).

- The lived experiences (for example, the way in which we judge a result of our performance may be influenced by what has already happened to us, or we observe that it happened to someone in the past).

- Expectations (for example, depending on what we expected to achieve, we can have a more or less motivating self-dialogue , which will undoubtedly influence our behavior).

Cognitive biases that 'fuel' negative internal dialogue

Most of our negative internal dialogue is the result of a misinterpretation of reality, which, in turn, can be the consequence of cognitive biases or distortions. Cognitive biases cause us to interpret reality partially, ignoring important elements of it, and altering basic cognitive functions such as attention (for example, we tunnel vision of what interests us), interpretation (for example, we take only part of reality, leaving aside other important data and reaching erroneous conclusions), and memory (for example, we erroneously store our lived experiences, as a result of a misinterpretation of them).

Among the most common cognitive biases we find:

- The magnification (for example, make too much of a negative fact or an error).

- The minimization (e.g., downplaying a positive or personal capacity, thinking that good things do not count).

- The catastrophism (for example, to anticipate everything that can go wrong).

- The overgeneralization (for example, think broadly as always, everything, nobody, etc., drawing universal conclusions).

- The divination of the thought (for example, believing that you know the reason for the behavior of the other, behaving towards him according to your self-dialogue, rather than to the true motives of the same).

All of them are associated with very intense emotions, which lead to behavior that is not very adjusted to the situation that triggers them. Learn to identify them and you will have taken the first step to stop your negative internal dialogue.

CHAPTER - 4

PAYING ATTENTION
TO PERFECTIONISM

In psychology, perfectionism consists of the belief that perfection can and must be achieved. In its pathological modality, it is the conviction that anything below an ideal of perfection is unacceptable.

Causes

Like most personality traits, perfectionism is familiar. It probably has a genetic component. Parents who combine authoritarian character with conditional love can contribute to perfectionism in their children.

Perfectionism can be an evolutionary legacy. The Hominids who were motivated for prolonged improvement and increases creating better tools. This gave them survival advantages.

Positive aspects

Perfectionism can channel success and provide motivation to persevere in the face of discouragement and obstacles. Roedell (1984) argues that "in a positive way, perfectionism can provide the driving energy that leads to great achievements. The meticulous attention to detail required for scientific research, the commitment that pushes composers to continue working until Music reflects the glorious sounds that sound in the imagination, and the persistence that keeps great artists before their easels until their creation matches their conception, all results from perfectionism ".

Slaney found that the levels of procrastination (postponement of activities) of the adapted perfectionists were lower than the prevailing levels in the non-perfectionists. Elite athletes, scientists, and artists frequently show signs of perfectionism. In childhood perfectionism is related to giftedness.

Negative aspects

In its pathological modality, perfectionism can be very harmful. It can manifest itself through procrastination , when used to postpone tasks ("I can't start work until I know the 'right' way to do it"), and self-loathing when used to excuse poor performance or to seek understanding and reinforcement from other people ("I can't believe I don't know how to reach my goals. How can I be unable to do this?").

In the workplace, perfectionism often becomes low productivity, as time and energy are wasted on irrelevant details of daily tasks or activities. This can lead to depression, peer antipathy, and an increased risk of accidents. Adderholt-Elliot describes five characteristics of perfectionist students and teachers that lead to poor performance:

- Procrastination.

- Fear to fail.

- All or nothing polarized thinking (see cognitive distortions).

- Crippling perfectionism.

- Work addiction.

In personal relationships, on both sides, unrealistic expectations can lead to great dissatisfaction. To try to achieve their goals, perfectionists often sacrifice family and social activities.

Therapists attempt to address the negative thinking inherent in perfectionism, particularly that relating to all or nothing, by which a result is thought to be either perfect or useless. They encourage their patients to set realistic goals and face their fear of failure.

CHAPTER - 5

CREATING

AFFIRMATIONS

5 steps you can take to create positive affirmations. These are the steps that I explain in the video and that I have been taking during this week, as part of the challenge of Week # 7 Attract the Life you Dream or # 100dreamdays. here is the worksheet for week # 7.

After the challenge of week 6 and working your internal voices, it is likely that you have detected many negative voices that prevent you from moving forward. Really, for a true change of life it is necessary to change some of the beliefs that keep you in your current state.

To do this, take advantage of the negative thoughts detected last week (those voices that tell you that you cannot, that you are worse or less capable than others, that it does not make sense or is not worth it...) and uses a technique of changing beliefs that I expose below.

STEPS TO CREATE YOUR OWN POSITIVE AFFIRMATIONS

Step 1

Ask yourself: Is this belief really true? Can I be 100% sure that this idea is completely real?

The normal thing is that you see that you cannot be 100% sure of the thoughts, these come and go; they change depending on our mood, circumstances, etc. So as soon as you verify that the belief is not absolutely true, go to the next step.

Step 2

Think about how you are and how you act when this belief is in you. You like what you see? Write down how you are and act with that belief.

Step 3

Ask yourself: who would you be without this belief? How would you act, how would you live if this belief were not part of your thinking?

Take time to reflect. Don't be in a hurry. Close your eyes and imagine without that belief. Then write it down.

Step 4

Remember if you ever acted without that belief. Maybe in another environment or in relation to other aspects of your life or a long time ago, even in your childhood.

Step 5

Finally write a positive phrase and contrary to your initial belief, based on your ability to be otherwise.

For example: if you think you are a person who does not dare to change, write in this last step: "I am a person who dares to make changes when they really need it."

The idea is that both one (negative) and the other (positive) beliefs may be true at any given time, but you choose which of the two will dominate your actions.

Do this exercise with as many limiting beliefs as you think necessary, to compile a list of new or empowering beliefs and have them in view.

I even recommend you write these enhancement phrases by hand and leave them in a visible place.

Read these phrases aloud once a day aloud. In this way you will gradually replace the old beliefs with the new ones. When you read these phrases or affirmations that you have created, do it with joy, conviction, although at first you do not believe it, imagine that it is so, that you are playing a character who thinks so.

Although in reality, it is totally true: you are playing your future character, the Self that you are going to become.

CHAPTER - 6

KNOW WHO YOU ARE

Without doubt, you are a wonderful being, full of light, with more attributes than you ever considered, essential for several people, interesting, with good intentions, with hundreds of virtues. This is a little difficult to see with our own eyes, especially if we are sad or depressed.

However, you need to look at your being from the perspective of another person, such as your partner, your mother, your best friend. They undoubtedly see you in a very different way. The most beautiful person in the world, the kindest, the one who is always present to listen, etc.

An excellent exercise you can do to strengthen your sense of being is to ask yourself who do I think I am? Surely you have never thought about it. If you dare, ask the people around you, what am I? They will be able to tell you an infinite number of adjectives that qualify you, from mother to tired, going from religious to overprotective, student or French, etc. You will realize that there are many ways to identify yourself as an individual.

It will undoubtedly be a lesson you will never forget. It is that the sense of yourself is what keeps you connected to the earth and determines what role you have assigned, what you are here for, etc. One of the first things to lose when we have a lot of work or are stressed is that connection, we forget what is really important in the path of self-realization and we increase the burden on our backs too much.

Life does not have to be this way, although it is true that mere mortals need to work, it is not the only thing that matters during our existence. It will give you more satisfaction to spend an afternoon with your children in the park than locked in the office doing overtime. They will appreciate it more.

Make a list with your attributes

Maybe you think that with a small piece of paper it will reach you to make a list of all your skills. That is not true at all. You have so many good things to write down that the sheet you have assigned for this exercise will not reach you.

Start the list in the most objective way possible, don't lie to yourself. Take into account your roles in society, your occupation, your religion, your nationality, your ethnic origin, your hobbies, your interests, your tastes, your activities, etc. Everything defines you as a human being and that can be seen by others just by seeing you or talking with you for a while.

But also, this list must contain the "internal" virtues, that which you know and those that surround you or frequent you often. Something describes you does not mean that it defines you, do not forget it. If at this moment you have a job as a market teller because the only thing that allows you to pay bills, do not write it down in the list, because it is not defining you, but it is a circumstance. What does define you is your love for music or for poetry, for example. Although you can also find something beyond your position, such as realizing that you like to talk to people, ask them how they are or even get a smile with a compliment. That is a virtue.

You must be honest with yourself on this list. No one has to see it, so don't lie to yourself. Not everything you write has to be flattering or a skill. If you are very jealous, fighter or nervous, also write it down. If you are overweight, too.

It is that a part of this work is to be able to fix or solve what can hurt you, both you and your loved ones or the next door neighbor. It is also necessary that you eliminate everything that does not contribute anything positive to your life, such as being an addiction (to tobacco, alcohol, work, etc.).

Perhaps you are even at a point where you cannot express what defines you with words, but with some specific action. It could be "I would never wear a yellow dress", "I always get lost in the supermarket parking lot", "I leave good tips in the restaurant", "I like to help animals", etc.

The right time to make this list is for you to decide. A good idea is that it is during the weekend, on your vacation or on a day off that you have. You don't have to put it together at a certain time or take a certain amount of time. Each one manages his emotions, his activities and his minutes in this life.

Once you have finished it (or so you think), store it in a place where you can see it whenever you want, such as on the nightstand or in the desk drawer. In a while, it is good to take a look at it to see what you have changed and if there is anything you can add. Sure you can remove an item (if you no longer smoke, if you stopped being so jealous with your partner, if you lost a few kilos, etc.).

Get to work as soon as possible with this list, which will allow you to change a lot as a person, be happier, go back to your origins, connect with what really matters and keep your feet firmly on the ground.

Why is it important to know yourself?

As I wrote before, because it is one of the fundamental pillars of your life. Getting to know you is the only way to know what you have for your personal self-realization, and it is the ideal way to know your skills, strengths and talents.

Knowing yourself is a direct way to analyze the aspects of yourself that you have to work on, improve or change, such as your fears, your weaknesses and your obstacles.

So instead of self-sabotaging, you strengthen yourself and make those weaknesses your allies.

It is important because knowing you contributes and increases your self-esteem. It is also important that you do not make the mistake of seeking to compare yourself with other people and seeking their approval, because this way will only lead you to dependency and away from yourself and from trusting yourself.

A second mistake to avoid is not to confuse "believing you don't know how to answer this question" with "fear of facing yourself." Don't confuse "who you are" with your life roles, either. For example, many people answer this question saying "I am a lawyer", "I am a mother", I am a doctor ", and this is not the point because being a doctor or being a mother are roles in life, it is not who you are.

If you were a doctor, you would be since you were born, or you were born as a mother. The answer to this question has to appeal to your essence, to what defines you, to what has been in you since you are, is what needs you, what makes you someone unique and unrepeatable.

CHAPTER - 7
FAMILY FACTOR

Valorization of education and parental supervision

The family got a decisive influence on the child's development. Parental attitudes and behaviors such as encouraging his child to study, congratulating him on his achievements, expressing tenderness, supervising him adequately, having high expectations and a positive attitude towards education, school and school tasks, being a model of parent-reader and participating in school life have positive effects on the young person's success.

PERSONAL FACTORS

Self-control and social and behavioral behaviors

Maintaining positive social interactions with peers and adults, having favorable social skills (empathy, mutual assistance, listening, etc.) and controlling one's impulses (self-control) is linked to academic success.

Association with peers

Vulnerable young people can be more easily influenced.

In this sense, the attendance of comrades motivated by the school will condition the attitude of young people towards their studies.

Diet and physical activity

The habits of life, fundamental for the development of the young person, his health, his self-esteem, as well as his personal and social development, are intimately linked to his educational success.

Tobacco-alcohol-drugs

The excessive use of tobacco, alcohol and drugs, which is harmful to the young person's general development, is also a predictive factor for dropping out of school, and even social.

Study-work balance

The work allows young people to get to know each other better, to acquire skills, to develop their autonomy as well as their sense of responsibility. However, the combination of activities (work, leisure, social activities, etc.) can lead young people to reduce the time spent on their studies, negatively influencing their results and their academic commitment.

Feeling depressed

Throughout their journey, young people may be brought to experience depressive episodes by the difficulties they face. Mental health problems, including depression, affect motivation and persistence in school.

Self esteem

Self-esteem is the awareness of the value that we recognize in different areas. A young person who has faith in his skills and abilities will not hesitate to engage in learning activities and to persevere.

Academic performance in reading, writing and math

Developing the pleasure and interest of reading and writing throughout life and responding to learning difficulties in these subjects as soon as they appear ensures greater chances of academic success.

Motivation and commitment

Poorly motivated students tend to adopt behaviors that are incompatible with learning and success at school, such as passivity, little effort and sloppy work, which can jeopardize their further studies.

School and professional aspirations

Students with well-defined academic and professional aspirations find the motivation necessary to persevere in their studies. Students with no specific school plan are more at risk of changing programs or dropping out of school.

SCHOOL FACTORS

Teacher-student relationship

The teacher has a major impact on students' perception of their skills and their academic performance. The quality of the relationship is all the more important for students exposed to the risk factors of dropping out (learning difficulties, disadvantaged environments, bad lifestyle habits, etc.).

Teaching and educational practices

Teaching practices, that is, what will be taught and how it will be done, have a major impact on student achievement, learning and eventual graduation.

Management practices

The management of an establishment acts as a catalyst within schools by taking concrete actions on a daily basis to promote student success.

Support for pupils in difficulty

The capacity of a school to intervene with a young person likely to drop out is important in the context of preventing school dropout. A young person in difficulty left to himself risks dropping out.

School climate

Establishing and maintaining a positive school climate is associated with better academic and social learning, better academic success and higher graduation rates.

SOCIAL FACTORS

Neighborhood of residence and neighborhood

The underprivileged districts, the remote rural areas and the sectors with high concentration of immigrants regularly face the problem of dropping out of school.

Community resources - community

Access to services and resources in the areas of housing, education, health, cultural and sporting activities, etc., which offer support to children, youth and their families, is a major issue. in the prevention of school dropout.

CHAPTER - 8

IDENTIFYING YOUR STRESSOR

Dramatize the concept of stress

Stress is mostly seen as negative. However, it is neither good nor bad in itself. To demonstrate this, I would like to share an analogy made by a guest (whose name I unfortunately did not remember) during a radio program, an analogy that I find particularly meaningful. It's about water. Imagine you are hiking in the middle of summer. It is very hot, the sun is burning and your water bottle is empty. Dehydration is waiting for you. You see a bungalow on the side of the road and you stop to ask for some water. Your host hands you a large glass of cool water, which you hasten to drink gratefully. It gives you a second drink that you can easily swallow, even if the pleasure is less. You are no longer thirsty. Yet he hands you a third glass of water. You do not want to offend the person who welcomed you so kindly but you have all the trouble in the world to finish this glass, feeling almost indisposed. Like water, stress is essential for your survival and it has beneficial and stimulating effects on your performance. However, if you face too much stress over a long period of time, it becomes harmful.

The stress mechanism

Stress is not an emotion. It is a reflex physiological and psychological reaction of the organism. This automatic mechanism was originally made to make you react to a danger by a physical action such as combat or flight. If these reactions were vital for the caveman when he had to run to save his skin in the presence of a wild beast, they are no longer adapted to the man of today. A priori, you rarely react physically to the multiple pressures of which you are the object. You will agree that it would be inappropriate to bump your manager or take your legs around your neck in the presence of an unhappy customer. As a result, the various "fuels" released into the blood in anticipation of

It was Hans Selye who first used the term "Stress" in the 1920s. Selye also introduced the concept of "general adaptation syndrome" (GAS), which describes the three successive reactions of the body when he faces a stressful situation. The initial phase of the process is the alarm phase: the person faces, but they use their energy resources to adapt to stress. Then comes the resistance phase: the individual persists in adapting to stress and resists but is under tension. Its energy resources are dwindling, the body has trouble recovering. If the stressful conditions persist or are linked without it being possible to recover comes the phase of: the situation has settled over time, the stress is permanent and becomes chronic. The person is exhausted physically and morally. Note that it is generally at this last stage that stress is referred to in everyday language.

Examples of exposure to risks and stressors

Overwork, lack of room for maneuver, contradictory orders, vague objectives, lack of resources... Examples of exposure to stressors (and psychosocial risks more generally) are numerous and can concern all sectors of activity.

Case of an employee in an administrative service

"In the morning, when I think about what to expect, it freaks me out already. I am constantly interrupted by people who ask me for information that I do not have, by colleagues who come into my office to consult files. My manager puts the files on the table at 6 p.m. so that I can finish them for the next day. And this software that I can't get to work ... I'm running. I am tired, I ruminate...".

This employee does not have sufficient resources to deal with the requests to which she must respond. She is in a state of chronic stress. The difficulties she encounters are linked to the organization and the nature of her work. The preventive measures could here relate to better work planning, an organization making it possible to concentrate requests for information at certain times of the day, or even training in the computer tools used.

Stress factors

The work-related stressors are the same as the

psychosocial risk factors. They are grouped into six large families.

- Work intensity and time: excessive work demands, work complexity, difficulties in reconciling professional and personal life...

- Emotional requirements: tensions with the public, obligation to hide their emotions...

- Lack of autonomy: overly rigid procedures, underuse of skills, etc.

- Degraded work social relationships: conflict between colleagues and / or management, lack of recognition, etc.

- Conflicts of values: ethical conflict (having to do things that you disapprove of), quality prevented (not having the means to do your job properly) ...

- Insecurity of the work situation: fear of losing your job, uncertainty about the future of your job...

IDENTIFY THE SOURCE OF YOUR WORK STRESS TO BETTER MANAGE IT

Stress is part of life. It is a natural reaction of the body, which releases specific hormones when it is necessary to adapt to certain situations. But its perception depends on many individual factors.

One can experience temporary work stress. Some will find it positive and stimulating, others, on the contrary, will see it as a counterproductive aggression. The peculiarity of this stress is that when its object disappears, everything returns to normal.

The most insidious is the permanent, diffuse stress, that which gnaws exhausts and which ends up causing significant havoc on health. If you want to break the vicious circle in which you feel trapped, and manage to manage your stress at work, you must know the causes.

KNOWING THE CAUSES OF STRESS AT WORK HELPS FIGHT IT TO FIND SERENITY.

Everyone reacts to stress variously, depending on their education, personality, past experiences or their environment. However, the researchers identified four elements, common to all, that trigger the release of stress hormones. You have surely been confronted with it:

1. When the situation eludes you: overwork or too much complexity of the work, unattainable objectives,

2. When you are faced with the unexpected: material or human failure, changing objectives, profession where nothing can be planned in advance,

3. When you have to do something unknown: adaptation to new tools, new responsibilities, and intervention in public,

4. When you feel threatened in your ego or your skills: an audit of your position, rivalry with a colleague.

Try to understand

The goal is to unravel the elements of your stress:

understand the mechanisms, decipher stressful situations, and identify their triggers. Do it in writing, calmly:

- Identify, among these factors, those that concern you right now,

- make an exhaustive list of places, times, situations, people, tasks... that put you in a state of anxiety,

- then ask yourself the reasons why you perceive them as threats.

Get back on top

This exam allows you to step back and reconsider, in a lucid manner, the importance that you attach to these facts that cause your anxiety. In the future, when you recognize them, you can adapt your reaction and reduce your stress.

But there is no miracle cure, and this reflection can be the occasion to change some reflexes.

Practice some good habits

On the work side:

- know how to recognize real emergencies, optimize your schedule, set yourself times to consult your emails and respond immediately only to those who have priority,

- learn to say no and know how to explain it without aggressiveness,

- communicate, seek the information you need from your colleagues,

- Take short breaks, to breathe, walk a little, do some exercises.

Personal side:

- adopt a healthy lifestyle: healthy eating, reduction of stimulants (tobacco, alcohol ...), restful sleep,

- consult your doctor if you need help,

- take a break from work on weekends to spend time with family and friends,

- Look for leisure activities to recharge your batteries: outings, sport.

CHAPTER - 9

ACTING ASSERTIVELY

It is important that we be assertive in our interactions with ADHD sufferers. For this, you must know what strategy and style of communication, assertiveness is differentiated and is located between two other polar behaviors: aggressiveness and passivity (or non-assertiveness).

Assertiveness is usually defined as mature communicational behavior in which the person neither attacks nor submits to the will of other people, but expresses their convictions and defends their rights. It allows defending the rights of each one without attacking or being attacked.

For Renny Yagosesky, Writer and Behavior Coach, Assertiveness is a complex category, linked to high self-esteem, which can be learned as part of a broad process of emotional development. He defines it as a form of conscious, consistent, clear, direct and balanced expression, the purpose of which is to communicate our ideas and feelings or defend our legitimate rights without the intention of hurting, acting from an internal state of self-confidence, instead of limiting emotionality typical of anxiety, guilt or anger. It also states that assertiveness is necessary and convenient for the benefits it generates.

The three Styles

To distinguish between the three concepts, it is helpful to understand how people manage their personal limits, as well as those of others.

Passive or non-assertive communicators tend not to defend their personal limits, and so allow aggressive people to influence them to the point of wrongdoing or even harm them. They are also typically reluctant to risk trying to influence someone.

The aggressive people tend not to respect the personal boundaries of others, and then they are forced to harm others while trying to influence them.

A person communicates assertively when he is not afraid to say what he thinks or tries to influence others, but does so in a way that respects the personal limits of others.

Main points of the assertiveness continuum:

Passive style - Assertive style - Aggressive style

One of the reasons why people are not very assertive is because they think they are not entitled to their beliefs, rights or opinions. In this sense, assertive training does not consist in turning submissive people into complainers and accusers, but rather to teach that people have the right to defend their rights in situations that are clearly unfair.

Assertiveness allows you to act, think and say what you believe to be the most appropriate for yourself, defending your rights, interests or needs without attacking anyone, or allowing yourself to be attacked. This is done without anxiety. Assertiveness is not synonymous with selfishness or stubbornness, but the right to express one's opinion, although it is possible that one is not right, and respecting the rights or points of view of others.

Assertiveness is an intermediate or neutral attitude between a passive or inhibited attitude and another aggressive attitude towards other people, which in addition to being reflected in spoken language is manifested in non-verbal language, such as in body posture, gestures or gestures of the body, facial expression, and voice. An assertive person is usually tolerant, accepts mistakes, proposes feasible solutions without anger, is self-confident, and peacefully restrains people who verbally attack them.

Assertiveness does prevent us from being manipulated by others in any aspect and is a decisive factor in preserving and increasing our self-esteem, in addition to valuing and respecting each other reciprocally.

Assertiveness is one of the social skills that can be taught by psychotherapists and personal development experts, and it is also the focus of many self-help books.

It is linked to self-esteem and considered an important social communication skill.

There are many techniques to be assertive. One of the techniques that work is to disarm the other before with a compliment or acknowledgment of their work, their person or their task, and then move on to express what we need. They defend their own rights (right to ask for help and express opinions) without violating the rights of the other, since there is no order, contempt or aggressiveness towards the other person. To be assertive is to express our points of view respecting that of others.

Other assertive techniques or behaviors are:

They are the set of ways to apply this technique, since there are many ways to apply it and for each interlocutor one can have a better result than the other:

Positive assertiveness

This form of assertive behavior consists of expressing genuine affection and appreciation for other people. Positive assertiveness assumes that one is attentive to what is good and valuable in others and, having realized this, the assertive person is willing to generously recognize what is good and valuable and communicate it verbally or non-verbally.

Empathetic assertiveness

Empathetic assertiveness allows us to understand, understand and act based on the needs of my interlocutor, in the same way it enables us to be understood and understood.

Confronting assertiveness

Assertive confrontational behavior is useful when we perceive an apparent contradiction between the words and deeds of our interlocutor. Then it describes what the other said he would do and what he actually did; then what you want is clearly expressed. With serenity in voice and words, without a tone of accusation or condemnation, you have to limit yourself to inquiring, asking questions, and then directly expressing a legitimate desire.

First person statements

The procedure is to describe the unwanted behavior of the other; express the negative feeling it causes us; explain the desired behavior; discuss the beneficial consequences of the desired change and, if it does not occur, the negative consequences of such a possibility. And all this with objectivity and serenity in words, gestures and tone of voice.

Fog bank

Another suggested technique is the Fog Bank, which consists of finding some limited point of truth in which you can agree with what your antagonist is saying. Expressly stated, you can agree in part or agree in principle.

Negative question

The negative question is to ask for further development into a statement or statements critical content from someone else. The objective is to get to see if it is a constructive or manipulative criticism.

The author Rivero Hernández, M. (2000) also proposes other techniques such as:

Selectively ignore

When in a discussion the other person insists on mixing topics that are not related to the central aspect of the discussion, those topics are ignored and only answered when it comes to the topic of interest.

Disarm anger or anger

It consists of refusing to argue with an annoying or uncomfortable person while in that state.

Classify problems

In a conversation or discussion, you should deal with only one topic at a time and not move on to another without having exhausted it.

Assertive agreement

It is fair, it is recognized that a mistake has been made, but without evaluating ourselves for that.

Process change

Shift the focus of the matter towards the analysis of what happens between you and your interlocutor, leaving aside the topic that apparently caused the discussion.

Process breakdown

Respond to provocative criticism with laconic phrases: Yes. No, perhaps, etc.

CHAPTER - 10
HEALTHY COPING

Mechanisms for a healthy coping with the difficulties of everyday life

Worry is defined as the fear that something will go wrong and it is something that affects everyone; although not equally; that is to say, everyone worries from time to time; But worrying all the time can be harmful, since it makes us feel tension, anxiety and suffering that prevents us from paying attention to other important things, paralyzing us and hindering our ability to think and plan.

Worry when it is not persistent over time is a positive thing, worrying is beneficial if it helps us prevent or solve a problem, to be better prepared, or ultimately, when it mobilizes us, it is a useful way of being prepared in the face of a threat.

Worries can become very absorbing and become the center of our lives, it is easy to fill life with small worries. We must not forget that it is something that is also learned by repeating or imitating role models; that is, sometimes we worry because from childhood we have learned to be alert to dangerous events and other times we have learned it automatically because one of our parents worried, easily when faced with problems.

CHAPTER - 11

ILLUSTRATE YOUR EMOTIONS

The emotional condition of the patient or the physiotherapist has a major influence on the physiotherapeutic care process. In a series of four articles we focus on successively 'general aspects', 'being afraid', 'being angry', and 'being sad'.

• Emotions within a physiotherapeutic setting.

• Being 'scared' within a physiotherapeutic setting.

• Anger placed within a physiotherapeutic setting.

• Sadness within a physiotherapy setting.

The importance of emotions is easily illustrated by the communication between the patient and the physiotherapist. What the physiotherapist tells and the way in which he does this can cause the patient to worry or to reassure him. Anxiety in the patient can cause him to misunderstand, misunderstand or withhold information from the physical therapist.

Another example of the influence that emotions can

have is the role played by the mutual relationship and treatment between a physiotherapist and the patient. The physiotherapist wants the patient to do, change or omit things. Emotions influence the entire process from being open, understanding, willing and able, to doing and continuing to do.

EMOTIONAL INTELLIGENCE

Physical therapists must have enough emotional intelligence to deal with the patient's own emotions and those. Emotional intelligence includes:

- Recognize and express. The physical therapist can recognize and name feelings in himself and in the other person. He can express his own feelings. He knows how to respond empathically to the other person's feelings.

- Regulate. The physical therapist has the ability to regulate his own feelings and knows how to influence the patient's feelings.

- Utilize. The physical therapist knows how to use the previous emotional skills functionally within the physiotherapeutic care process.

What emotions are you talking about?

There are five basic emotions: three negative (scared, angry and sad) and two positive (joy and affection). These basic emotions can be further nuanced on the basis of the intensity, duration and situation. Being "afraid" ranges from mild anxiety to chronic anxiety and panic. "Anger" from mild irritation to anger and "sadness" from slight disappointment and pity to heartbreaking sorrow.

The positive emotions can also be nuanced. "Joy" moves between light cheerfulness and ecstasy or euphoria. Affection ranges from sympathy and affection to deeply touching love.

The mutually different emotions carry different degrees of activation. Emotions that have a high degree of activation (fear and anger) will cause physiological symptoms that are unfavorable for recovery. Consider, for example, an increase in muscle tone, less coordinated movement and an ergo trophic vegetative climate.

That is not to say that other emotions do not affect health. For example, grief causes reduced immune function. Happiness, on the other hand, is associated by researchers with a range of positive health effects. The physiotherapist can influence recovery favorably if he reduces negative affect, but also if he can induce positive affect.

ROLE OF EMOTIONS IN PHYSIOTHERAPY

The context in which emotions play a role between patient and physiotherapist falls within one of the following three themes:

- health treatment;

- treatment of a patient physiotherapist;

- life events (work / private).

By combining each of the five basic emotions with each

of the three contexts, a matrix can be created - both for the patient and for the physiotherapist - that provides insight into the panorama of emotionality within the physiotherapeutic context.

Examples of the context 'health treatment' can be: the patient is afraid that he is permanently limited; the physical therapist becomes irritated when it appears that 'nothing' helps. The context 'treatment of the patient-physiotherapist' can be seen from the following: the patient is sad (disappointed) that the physiotherapist does not keep his appointment. Or: the physiotherapist cherishes friendly feelings towards the patient.

Examples of life events that can affect: the patient is angry because his employer has hurt him, or the physical therapist is concerned that the waiting list will grow even further.

Elements in emotions

It is not possible to explain exactly what an emotion is, but one can name a number of elements within this complex experience.

- The first element that we mention is 'evolution'. Human emotional expression is strikingly similar to that of certain animals. In addition, basic emotions are found in all cultures. All over the world, a smile is recognized as a smile.

- Second, emotions are often experienced physically. In fact, William James argued that the emotional experience is nothing more than perceiving and interpreting the bodily sensations that arise in certain situations.

- Biology is a third element. Especially the phylogenetic old brain structures, such as the limbic system, are involved in emotions. Conditioning can cause fears without the intervention of the cerebral cortex. As a result, a patient cannot always express why he is afraid. The neocortex usually also plays a role. The left anterior frontal lobe is more activated with positive emotions, the right with negative emotions. This explains why the emotionality in stroke patients may have changed. Moreover, this 'lateralization of emotion' explains why unexplained physical complaints, which are often related to negative emotions, are more often experienced in the left half of the body.

- Learning certainly belongs to the elements that play a role in the phenomenon of 'emotion'. The combination of emotion and learning can be divided into two aspects. First, the 'classical conditioning'. An example of this is a patient who repeatedly gets pain and therefore fear when climbing stairs. In the long run, seeing the stairs is enough to evoke fear. We call the second aspect 'operant conditioning'. The same patient sees the stairs and feels the fear; he decides to take the elevator so that the fear is gone immediately. Avoiding stairs is "rewarded" with a reduction in anxiety.

- As the last element of emotion we mention the cognitions. The 'philosophical spectacles' through which people view the world largely determine the experience of emotions. Some people are not irritated by the same incident, while others almost blow themselves up with anger.

- The influence of culture on emotions can manifest itself through conditioning and cognitive learning.

Cognitions and emotions

People judge or interpret events as harmful, neutral or positive for their interests, resulting in matching emotions. If the patient believes that the pain during exercise is due to damage occurring, he will become afraid and careful. When interpreting events, it is not only about physical, advantages or disadvantages of an event, but often also about the psychological. For example, the loss of self-esteem in physical mutilation is usually more painful than the mutilation itself. In addition, people assess whether they have the resources, skills and energy to do something about the threat (coping). After all, a threat that you can easily ward off will hardly cause any emotional turmoil.

Deep-seated needs

A very pervasive need, which can explain much of the behavior, thinking and emotions, is the need 'to belong' (need-to-belong). It is a strong (innate) need to enter into and maintain long-term, positive and significant interpersonal relationships. Other motives, such as self-presentation, performance and being nice, can be deduced from this. If that need is met, it is experienced as a positive mood, and physical and psychological health. Deprivation of that need leads to negative affect, such as sadness, disappointment, fear and feelings of loneliness and inferiority.

Our behavior is often driven by such deeper needs and interests. As a result, unexpected emotions can sometimes arise in the patient during apparently insignificant incidents.

REBT

The cognitive model of emotions predicts that when a person's view or evaluation of the situation changes, so will his emotions and behavior. This is confirmed in research. In particular, it is Albert Ellis' Rational Emotive Behavior Therapy (REBT) that seizes the evaluation of events to change emotions. In his view, there are four categories of evaluative cognitions that greatly increase emotions in duration and severity.

- With 'mustism' one demands something in which one can in fact only have a preference. The physical therapist demands that the patient exercise well and is severely disappointed if this is not the case.

- In 'catastrophizing' one turns a mosquito into an elephant: the patient finds the pain of the light sprain very terrible.

- With 'low frustration tolerance', people tell themselves that they absolutely cannot tolerate discomfort. The physiotherapist says that he cannot tolerate 'nagging' patients; the patient says that he cannot continue the exercises.

- In 'value judgments' one assesses and condemns oneself, the other or 'the world'. It is also outrageous that those doctors strike.

We can also turn things around: if a patient or a physiotherapist is violently or long emotionally, he will undoubtedly have one or more of the above evaluative cognitions.

The emotional response

The physical therapist must take into account that emotions have a profound effect on the total person: thinking, feeling, doing, as well as the accompanying physiology.

Emotion requires expression. Some people don't express their emotions enough. This is very unfavorable both for contacts with others and for physical and mental health. If the patient does not express himself, care providers may underestimate or miss the emotion. It is therefore advisable for the physiotherapist to explicitly inquire whether there are any issues that are of great concern to the patient.

It is extremely beneficial for the well-being and health of the patient if he is encouraged to tell his story to a physiotherapist who knows how to listen. This opening-up has an effect on subjective disease measures, such as the reported pain, and on objective disease measures, such as the degree of joint inflammation in rheumatism and the 1-second value in asthma.

Emotions and stigma

Many chronically ill have been stigmatized. A stigma arises from fear of deviating from what culture defines as 'normal'. One judges the deviant with matching emotions of anger, disgust, fear, and so on. To protect themselves, both the lay person and the rescuer reduce or avoid contact with the stigmatized. The stigmatized person becomes isolated, the value judgment feels depressed and this negative self-image takes over. This creates sadness, disappointment, fear and tension. The misery this entails, for example, leads to a dramatically high suicide rate in AIDS.

Emotions and 'talking about it'

The more intense an emotional event, the more one tends to talk about it. This is part of the main reasons why patients often tell their personal ups and downs to the physiotherapist and the physiotherapist in turn tells the story, if it affects him, to colleagues at work or to the partner at home. This human trait runs counter to professional secrecy.

Voting and information processing

A pleasant mood, for example within therapy, promotes creative thinking and problem solving. Moreover, a patient is then easier to convince. These beliefs are less durable because they did not originate from a thorough cognitive assessment process. There is something to be said about tempering an overly cheerful patient so that he thinks more seriously about the advantages and disadvantages of an important advice.

Emotion draws information processing in a certain direction. Anxiety is more likely to cause danger, while a depressed mood makes it easier for the patient to see and remember all kinds of misery. A circular process can then arise. As a physiotherapist you can take into account that your own mood or that of the patient colors the judgment, for example about the degree of effort during the therapy.

Culture and emotions

Each culture ensures, through its specific values and norms, that different emotion are experienced in the same situation. Western society attaches great importance to autonomy, individual achievements, power and status. As a result, curtailment thereof can quickly lead to negative emotions. In many Eastern cultures, on the other hand, the individual is perceived as subordinate to the whole (the group, for example). One does not perceive 'putting oneself at service' as a 'sacrifice' but as a realization of a deep value (31). For example, the well-intentioned encouragement of the physiotherapist that 'sports will make you look more attractive' or the remark 'that you have to think about yourself' may be highly valued in one culture, but not in another.

The functions of emotions

Emotions reveal that there is a central interest in the game. Moreover, emotions place that importance at the center of consciousness. Emotions take precedence. It is difficult to get around. They guide our choices and behavior and prepare the body in a physiological sense for the actions to be taken. Social interaction is also largely driven by emotions. We notice from the other person what we should or shouldn't say or do. In addition, positive and negative emotions are used socially and culturally in 'socialization' to educate the participants of the group or culture through appropriate views, attitudes and behavior through reward and punishment.

Train skills

In the eyes of the patient, one in five physiotherapists performs below expectations on explanation of the complaint and listening behavior. More attention to psychosocial aspects or counseling and to the significance of disorders and limitations for the patient is desirable. Care providers often do not know the (psychosocial) agenda that the patient brings with him. Fortunately, students can successfully train in the complex communication skills required to guide emotional states. Attention for a more person-oriented attitude is important here, otherwise the listening behavior will remain below par and the psychosocial component will not be picked up from the patient's complaint.

It is important for the physiotherapist to deal with emotions. Physical therapists have a risk of eventually becoming burned out (burnout) due to emotionally stressing patients and their inability to cope with this. Burnout is characterized by:

- emotional exhaustion;

- depersonalization (negative distant approach to the patient);

- reduced personal ability within the workplace.

- What should the physiotherapist be able to do

The physical therapist must recognize for himself and the patient:

- whether there is an emotion;

- what emotions are at play;

- what the intensity of the emotions is;

- what the emotion relates to;

- Whether the emotions do have an impact on the physiotherapy care process;

- if appropriate, guide the patient in this.

Characteristic conversation situations

Basic emotions can be taken as the starting point for teaching complex communication skills. Some typical conversation situations are:

Anxious:

- calm and reassure the patient,

- guiding fear of movement in the patient;

Angry:

- Receiving criticism from the patient / dealing with errors.

- Criticize.

- To deal with aggression;

Sad:

- the bad news conversation,

- dealing with loss and grief;

- joy and affection:

- dealing with patient and self-boundaries,

- Affection, distance and proximity.

We must not forget that it is something that is also learned by repeating or imitating role models; that is, sometimes we worry because from childhood we have learned to be alert to dangerous events and other times we have learned it automatically because one of our parents worried, easily when faced with problems.

CHAPTER - 12
FREE YOURSELF FROM GUILT AND SHAME

More and more people share what they have experienced. Now that this is open, more and more stories and experiences emerge. And yes... unfortunately there is a lot of sexual abuse and violence. It turns out. We can't get around that. And ooh, how often that has been hidden for a long time.

OUR SEX AWARENESS IS GROWING

The sharing of experience stories has a great effect. In the first place, of course, for those involved. This also has an effect on our society. A conversation has started about sexuality, boundaries and sex perception. People think about their own experiences. About their own behavior. Men as well as women. Perpetrators and victims. The impact of unwanted behavior on someone's life is poignantly visible. Our consciousness grows as a result.

A WOUND REQUIRES CARE

"In my work as a Gestalt therapist I see how people struggle with their unpleasant experiences. I experience closely how much they suffer from this. Unfortunately, you cannot undo events that have hurt you. You can learn how to deal with your injuries so that the wound can heal. This is a process I regularly compare with inflammation in the skin. Because it is pleasant and reassuring to make a comparison with something that feels less heavy. Without, of course, downplaying or brushing away. Something happened that hurt you. What caused you an injury."

This hurts, perhaps terribly, very much. If such a wound is not properly cared for or covered too quickly, it can become inflamed. This is going to be a painful and nagging place. Red and swollen. It kindles and pus accumulates. This can take a long time and the tension of this place is constantly felt. You can hardly escape it. It determines your mood. It determines how you interact with others. It determines how you are in life. And then one pin prick may be enough to make an opening.

First comes the dirt... the pus. Everything comes out. Everything is allowed. In fact... everything must be removed for the wound to heal. When the wound receives the necessary attention and care, it can heal. However, the scars will remain visible and the spot can remain sensitive. This is also the case with mental injuries.

THE TIME IS NOW

And that is exactly what is happening now. There are more and more stories from people. More and more confessions are coming.

So much is coming out that there are even voices saying that the #metoo effect is breaking through. I don't think it is. We don't talk. It's like the pus that comes out when an inflammation opens. It is a collective discharge. Everything that is painful now appears.

The time is now. The opening is there. The stories may be heard. The secrets may be revealed. People are allowed recognition. Because only when the pain may be there. Only when we can speak openly about it. Only then can healing take place.

FREE YOURSELF FROM SHAME AND GUILT

In 2017, talking about sexuality, sex perception and sexual abuse is still largely shrouded in mist. A mist of judgment, guilt and shame. How many people keep their mouth shut because they feel ashamed or guilty? Because sexuality is still a taboo. Because they think they made a mistake. Because they think it's their own fault. That they provoked something. But it is not your fault. Free yourself from guilt. Free yourself from shame. Your story is welcome and may be heard.

LEARN TO DEAL WITH SEXUAL ENERGY

The power and energy of sexuality is great. So great that urges can rule over common sense. That is why it is crucial we talk about this. That we learn how to channel this energy. What do you do with feelings of lust, for example? Can you have it? Is that the same for men and women? What are limits? How do you recognize it? How do you declare it? Can you enjoy sex?

I think it is of great value that discussions are now taking place on this. The stories that come forward through #metoo set this in motion. It is a revolution. Something is changing in our consciousness. There is a collective release from guilt and shame. Hoera! The more people talk concerning it, the more space is created.

When the pus is out, when the pain heals, the healthy conversation can start.

LET'S TALK ABOUT SEX BABY

This is how we, collectively, grow into a new consciousness. An awareness in which the experience of sex evolves. In which we teach our children to speak about this. This creates more space for the beauty of sexuality. After all, sex is the start of all our lives. Sexual energy is powerful. Sexual energy is creative and creative. I can write a lot about that, but now is not the time. Now the pain demands attention. Let's listen to each other. Let's talk. In openness. The tension has to go. The 'wound' wants to be cleared.

Do you feel that you are in pain and need your 'wound' care? Do not hesitate. Ask for help! Open your mouth and share it with the people and where you feel good. With friends or professionals. You can speak. You can free yourself. Now!

YOU ARE VALUABLE... BEHAVE ACCORDINGLY!

There is another aspect that is very important and that should certainly not be missing in this writing. That is about care and responsibility. By that I mean that you act with care and attention for yourself. That you take responsibility for your own happiness. You are valuable and deserve to be treated that way. You don't have to wait for others to do that. You can start immediately. So... hoppa! Take yourself seriously. Take the time to feel. What are your heart wishes? What is your heartache? What do you need now? Take your time. It is hard to feel this right.

STRENGTHEN YOUR OWN STRENGTH TO LEAVE VICTIMHOOD BEHIND

When you listen to yourself in this way and take yourself seriously, you strengthen your own strength. And this power is needed to leave the victimhood behind. Nobody else can do that for you. That is a choice you can make. This way you take control of your own life. And that is necessary so that you can do what you desire. Not because you have to. But because it is allowed. In freedom.

Teach people how to strengthen their own strength. How they can listen to the wisdom in themselves. How they connect to their hearts. Because your heart is a compass and shows you the way. Also when it comes to experience and questions about sexuality.

CHAPTER - 13
FORGIVENESS AND LESSON LEARNED

Do you frequently apologize? Saying "forgiveness", in principle, is one of those social cements that strengthen our relationships. However, doing it consistently can weaken self-esteem.

Pride, the trap of self-esteem

Personal integrity, a pillar of self-esteem

I don't like myself: what can I do?

The moment we apologize must be punctual and meaningful. It should not be a continuous, almost obsessive exercise that hints at our lack of confidence. Find out how to stop apologizing frequently.

While this could be a distinguishing feature of our politeness or our good upbringing, apologizing sometimes turns into a dynamic with negative implications for ourselves.

The same thing happens with forgiveness. We can say

this word twenty times a day, even forty. However, it is always better to use it when it is really needed. Let us think about this idea.

Do you frequently apologize?

When you apologize frequently, you make it clear to the other that he must release you from something. Sooner, the people around you will get tired. Or worse, will end up thinking that you don't have enough self-confidence to act in total autonomy. So, and as it happens in any area of life, everything extreme is bad. Whether we abuse something or totally forget it.

Take the example of Donald Trump. One of his most famous phrases is the one in which he says "never apologize because he is never wrong". Another example of this extreme is that of Martin Winterkorn, the former CEO of Volkswagen.

Even if the fraud committed in the emissions of its diesel cars has been largely proven, it took more than a year before apologizing publicly. By the time he did, the trust of many of his customers had already been shattered.

We devalue the purpose of forgiveness

Forgiving and asking for forgiveness are two extremely therapeutic exercises. They resolve conflicts, release weights, relieve tensions. Few acts involve greater responsibility than assuming one's involvement in an offense and asking the other to forgive us. However, if we spend our time saying sorry for minor things, the essence of the latter loses its importance.

We devalue ourselves

Do you keep asking for forgiveness? In this case, stop for a moment to think about the following idea. How do you think others view you each time you apologize for something that has no significance or repercussions? Certain situations do not justify the use of this word. Most of the time, no real circumstances required the need to be forgiven.

We must understand that asking for forgiveness all the time does not make us more humble, more correct or more respectful. Do not apologize for asking questions, sitting down, dropping this pen, asking for help, breathing ... Trust yourself and show that you have self-esteem.

Ask for forgiveness to get out of certain situations

Almost all of us do it: we apologize for getting out of certain situations. These moments reveal our insecurity or our shyness. Let's think about it. It is common to apologize when we speak to a stranger or someone in the hierarchy. "Sorry, can I ask you a question?" "," Excuse me, you could give me this fallen object ... ".

The problem lies here in the abuse of this word. Forgiveness becomes a problem when it turns into a persistent resource in our vocabulary, a gear that makes us move over a large part of our social terrain.

When to ask for forgiveness and when not to?

Do you frequently apologize? So you probably want to know when it's better to do it or not. Working on this aspect of our behavior will make us feel more competent and confident in any situation and on any terrain.

When to ask for forgiveness

· When you hurt someone

When you have offended, disappointed, or hurt a person's feelings

When you regret a behavior or an action performed

Be able to apologize each time you make a mistake and your mistake affects other people

When you want to close cycles to leave old grudges behind

Let us also try to ask forgiveness from ourselves. We all accumulate errors or inadequate choices which are heavy to bear and which deserve to be released, forgiven

When not to ask for forgiveness

Don't apologize when you give your opinion

Avoid saying this word in situations where it lacks meaning: when you are addressing someone, when you want to ask a question, when you need to take something...

Don't ask for forgiveness when you need help

Do you frequently apologize? Even if there are times when asking for forgiveness is necessary, in the majority of cases, we abuse this term when its use does nothing.

To conclude, even though we have heard that "asking for forgiveness does not make us stronger", we must understand that everything has limits. Sometimes abuse takes away the real and powerful meaning of this healthy term. And makes us lose all self-esteem. Let us use this wonderful word more appropriately and with more wisdom.

PART 3

OVERCOMING LOW SELF ESTEEM IN REAL LIFE

But what if you think so negatively about yourself that you cannot enjoy interacting with others, cannot work well and can no longer enjoy life?

Don't you like yourself enough? Or are you struggling with negative thoughts about yourself? Do you feel that you are doing everything wrong?

Chances are that you suffer from a negative self-image and that you are looking for ways to improve your self-image.

A negative self-image can be a big problem with harmful consequences for your mental health and your life. In this article you get the most important steps to improve your self-image!

What is a negative self-image?

The self-image is, as it were, the opinion you have about yourself.

A negative self-image therefore means that you have a negative opinion about yourself.

You judge yourself as not good or not good enough and would rather be different. You look up to others and wish you were just like them.

Just listen carefully to the way arrogant people speak about themselves. they are full of talk about their past achievements and what they will achieve in the future.

The opinion you have about yourself is very important because it determines what you consider yourself capable of. If you have a very positive image of yourself, you expect to be able to do a lot.

No one is born with boundless confidence and positive self-image. If someone seems to be incredibly confident, it's because they've been working on it for years.

While insecure people often keep a little more in the background and tend to think they cannot and will fail something.

The self-image is therefore a continuum with on the one hand a negative self-image and on the other extreme an (over) positive self-image.

Both extremes can lead to emotional and social problems.

Doing valuable activities strengthens our self-image. It confirms that we are good at something, because we have carried out successful activities.

Conversely, if you have a negative image of yourself, you will be less likely to engage in such valuable activities.

If you suffer from a negative self-image, you probably spend a lot of time thinking about your negative beliefs about yourself and see these ideas confirmed over and over again.

You relate events to yourself, when it is not always about you.

In contact with others, for example, you tend to think that everyone is watching you and is disapproving of you. Because of this you always have the idea that you fail and that others reject you.

You also quickly think that you are a burden to others and you quickly feel too much and unwelcome. In addition, you are likely to explain events in a negative way. Neutral statements are then interpreted as critical, when they were not meant to be.

To date, the negative self-image is not a psychiatric diagnosis, but does appear to be an underlying problem in various disorders.

CAUSES OF A NEGATIVE SELF-IMAGE

Some common causes are:

CAUSE 1: NEGATIVE PARENTS OR CAREGIVERS

The basis of your self-image forms in childhood and develops over the course of your life into an extensive complex of ideas.

Ideally, parents encourage their children to develop a positive self-image. They do this by always admiring and complimenting their children.

Just think of the praise of parents when they receive the drawings and artworks from their children.

Objectively, it is often not that special, but parents react as if they have never seen anything so beautiful. This kind of admiration is essential for forming a positive self-image.

Some parents are not very capable of this, for example because they are not so stable themselves, because they are not home enough or because they have very high demands on their child.

In such a case, instead of praise, a child is criticized and cannot learn that he is worthwhile.

CAUSE 2: NEGATIVE PEERS

During childhood and early adolescence, peers have a great influence on which you are.

Risk factors for developing a negative self-image include staying with a group of peers you don't accept as you are who hurt and humiliate you.

Or forcing you to do things you don't want and don't take your ideas and feelings seriously.

Bullying is the most extreme form of this, but even if you do not have many friends or are always chosen last with the gym, this can have a negative impact on the development of your self-image.

You can then get the impression that something is wrong with you and that other people don't like you the way you are.

CAUSE 3: TRAUMA

This can involve various types of trauma, from abuse to sexual abuse to neglect.

You often see that people who have experienced such trauma suffer from post-traumatic stress disorder (PTSD).

These kinds of experiences can damage your self-image, as it were.

You can start thinking that you don't deserve respect and that you yourself are to blame for what happened to you.

CAUSE 4: IMAGING IN THE MEDIA

Today, we are constantly surrounded by images of beautiful and slender people who seem perfect in many ways.

Just think of the advertisements with photoshopped

models, or all successful stories and photos on Facebook.

It seems that others are always beautiful and intensely happy.

Because we constantly compare each other with other people, you can quickly get the impression that you are less beautiful, fun and perfect than others.

CAUSE 5: NEGATIVE THOUGHT PATTERNS

The longer you think, talk or feel about yourself in a certain way, the more this way of thinking wears off.

This can create a pattern in which you criticize yourself.

This way of thinking will become more and more automatic until you lose control of it at some point.

After which it will dominate an increasingly larger area of your life. The negative thought pattern is besides a causal factor also a factor that perpetuates the problem.

CHARACTERISTICS OF A NEGATIVE SELF-IMAGE

People with a negative self-image are found in all layers of society.

These can be very different persons who have little in common.

However, there are a number of characteristic symptoms that almost everyone with a negative self-image suffers from.

Yet it is important to be aware that there is also a group of people with whom it is sometimes more difficult to recognize.

These are people who try to shout out their insecurity and pretend to be tougher and more confident than they feel inside.

Below are some of the characteristic behaviors that can help you identify a negative self-image:

SOCIAL WITHDRAWAL

Because you have little self-confidence on the interpersonal level, you often suffer from social anxiety.

Social interactions are difficult and uncomfortable, because you feel shy, everyone seems to look at you and think that you will go off again.

This gives you the chance to experience anxiety disorders such as agoraphobia or a social phobia.

The barrier to go among people is getting higher and you will withdraw more and more.

CAN'T SAY NO

Because you really care about the opinion of others, you have trouble saying no.

This makes you more likely to agree with the plans of others, even if you don't really want to.

AVOID CONFLICTS

If the opinion of others is very important to you, you will of course do everything you can to avoid conflicts.

INDECISION

Because you have little confidence in your own insight

and skills, you have serious doubts when making decisions.

EXAGGERATING OFTEN TO MAKE EXCUSES

People with negative self-esteem tend to say sorry often, even if they can't help themselves.

In everything that goes wrong, you assume that you are the cause.

ATTRIBUTE SUCCESSES TO OTHERS OR TO HAPPINESS

If something has gone well, you tend to think that this success is not due to your actions, but to others or environmental factors.

DIFFICULTY ACCEPTING COMPLIMENTS

Because you think so negatively about yourself, you will not easily believe that someone else has a positive impression of you.

This will make it difficult to deal with compliments.

You respond, for example, by denying it, by attributing the success to someone else, or by thinking that the person is laying.

The consequences of a negative self-image

As you understand by now, a negative self-image has a large, negative impact on almost all aspects of your life.

It causes a constant stream of criticizing thoughts in which you see yourself as less good, fun, nice, attractive and competent than others.

To get rid of these annoying thoughts, try to pretend to be different from what you are. For example, you imitate the behavior of people you consider popular or successful.

However, you will soon notice that this does not help and that you fall by the wayside because you are performing a kind of play.

You have entered a negative spiral; in your mind you feel a loser, you try to appear competent, but because of your negative self-image this fails, which makes you think about yourself even worse.

A negative self-image can also make you feel that you don't matter in this world.

When you are among the people you can feel lonely and feel that you don't belong there.

Sometimes it can seem as if you are invisible, as it were, and nobody even notices you. You keep a little in the background and do not dare to take much initiative to contact.

It can even be so bad that you feel that you are not really connected to the people you associate with.

For example, friends sometimes seem to take advantage of you and you seem to be less important to them than their other friends. This feeling of unimportance can get so bad that you start to withdraw and eventually become depressed.

In your life you encounter various problems in various

situations because you are not assertive. You tolerate others treating you in an unpleasant way.

You don't feel valuable and don't expect others to treat you this way. This way you can get a partner who doesn't take good care of you, who cheats or abuses you.

Instead of standing up for yourself you think "they are right" and let it get over you. These unpleasant experiences can in turn reinforce the negative image of yourself.

Furthermore, a negative self-image has a lot of influence on the choices you make in your life, such as your choice of study, choice of partner, career choice, hobbies etc.

Because if you think that you are not as good as others and that everything that comes out of your hands will fail, you will not put much thought into making your future plans.

It often starts in puberty, a time when most of us have little confidence in ourselves.

For example, adolescents with low self-esteem think they are not smart enough for a particular education or study and step in a level lower.

Then they get a job below their level. At work you underestimate yourself and feel inferior to others.

Colleagues are running over you, letting you do the trick and you may even end up in annoying situations where there is sexual harassment.

All this then confirms the negative image that you already had of yourself and so you get stuck in a vicious circle that further strengthens itself.

Hobbies are activities in which you become relaxed by doing something and stop thinking for a while. Unfortunately, a negative self-image can also be a disturbing factor here.

The negative self-image can shift the focus from performing the activity to negative thoughts about yourself and your performance.

People with low self-esteem often avoid competitive sports and activities that put them in the spotlight.

First of all, this does not encourage you to develop certain talents.

In addition, because you keep more in the background, you have less chance of being discovered. For example, imagine that you can sing very well.

A confident person might sign up to participate in X-factor and win a great record deal there. But with a negative self-image nothing would come of this.

You probably wouldn't sign up anyway.

And if you did register, you would feel so insecure during the rehearsals and doubt yourself so much that your performance would fail terribly.

You are therefore doomed to sing in the bathroom where no one can hear you.

NEGATIVE SELF-IMAGE IN ADULTS

A negative self-image can arise in childhood or during puberty. Puberty is a time when most young people feel insecure about who they are and what they are capable of.

This makes a negative self-image less noticeable.

However, a large proportion of young people grow over it again during adulthood. In another part, however, it remains. So the basis for a negative self-image can lie in childhood or adolescence.

Scientifically Proven: onion t a survey conducted in 48 countries showed that the self-image from adolescence to always be positive in adulthood. The highest positive peak would be around the age of 60.

But with age, positive self-esteem diminishes, presumably due to changes in financial status and increasing physical limitations.

Improve negative self-image? 8 tips

Having a negative self-image has far-reaching and unpleasant consequences for the course of your life.

Fortunately, the opinion you have about yourself is not static and can change over the course of your life.

After all, you often change your mind! Below are tips on how to tackle a negative self-image and ensure that you start thinking positively about yourself.

TIP 1: BECOME AWARE OF THE NEGATIVE JUDGMENTS ABOUT YOURSELF

Assessing yourself negatively may have become such an automated process over the years that you may not even be aware of it.

A first step is therefore to consider this. Listen carefully to that little voice in your head that always criticizes everything.

What are the things you say to yourself?

TIP 2: CHALLENGE YOUR NEGATIVE THOUGHTS

However convinced you may be of your negative thoughts, you realize that a negative self-image is nothing more than an opinion.

Therefore, try to examine as objectively as possible to what extent your opinion is correct.

Try to actively collect evidence that you are good, fun and successful!

TIP 3: SPEAK HELPING THOUGHTS

Instead of listening to the constant criticism of that little voice in your head, you express positive thoughts.

Whenever you find yourself criticizing yourself, you have a neutral or positive thought.

You keep repeating this thought over and over again, causing the annoying voice to lose its stage.

You will notice that the more you do this, the more you start to believe in it yourself.

TIP 4: SMILE MORE OFTEN

It's a small thing that can cause a chain reaction.

When your person smiles, it affects certain muscles in the body that make you feel happy.

TIP 5: RECALL POSITIVE MEMORIES OF PAST SUCCESSES

Think back to a kind of situation where you were very successful.

Try to imagine this memory down to the smallest details and to recall the feeling of the past.

Think about where you were, what you did, what clothes you were wearing, and adopt the same posture and facial expression.

Do this five times a day and expand your repertoire of memories as much as possible.

You can also do it at work, for example at the coffee machine or if you look out the window.

TIP 6: GIVE YOURSELF A PEP TALK IN THE MIRROR

It may sound silly but speaking to yourself while looking in the mirror will boost your confidence!

Say things to yourself like "I'm worth it" or "I'm a nice person".

Try to say it with as much conviction as possible and also evoke the corresponding feeling.

TIP 7: DO NOT COMPARE YOURSELF TO OTHERS

Many people with a negative self-image always compare themselves with others and then have a poor evaluation.

Stop this!

Every person is unique and does things in his own way, which makes every individual so special.

Tip 8: Reversing negative self-image for good?

With these tips you are already a long way to work on your self-image. Still having trouble with negative thoughts about yourself and want to learn...

How can you stop being so hard on yourself?

How can you deal with negative emotions more easily?

How can you motivate yourself instead of being critical?

Then I now have the solution for you. A negative self-image is associated with low self-confidence. This means it can affect your whole life, from how you behave in relationships to how you project yourself at work.

23 PRACTICAL OR EXERCISES FOR SELF-ESTEEM CHILDREN

1. Laugh together

Laughter relaxes and makes life seem much easier. This will benefit not only your child but your entire family.

That's why laughs as much as possible. Children laugh a lot more than adults anyway - let yourself be infected. Above all, dealing with minor misfortunes in a hilarious manner helps your child to deal with mistakes in a more relaxed manner.

Very important:

Laughs together - but never over each other.

NEVER laugh at your child! To be laughed at is the worst.

What you can do to your child's self-esteem.

2. Small rituals

Rituals provide security and trust. A child who does feel safe and secure is not easily thrown off the track by difficulties. At the same time, it learns to stick to regular habits. It can then use this ability later on, for example, to exercise regularly.

How about a morning ritual, for example?

Instead of starting the day carelessly and maybe even in a bad mood, I recommend 5 minutes of "pee-long stocking time" every morning: In these 5 minutes everything that is silly, crazy and funny is allowed: bounce, tickle, make faces, make funny noises, sing loudly, pillow fight or whatever else you can think of. Your child will have a lot of great ideas. Give it a try. You will be amazed at how positive and lively this will start not only your child, but also yourself!

Quiet rituals are more appropriate for the evening.

The classic and popular with all children is the bedtime story. So that you don't have to constantly buy new books, I have collected a lot of great stories for you: 400 good night stories.

Or you can just let your child fall asleep with a mental story every night. In this way, positive suggestions can be anchored directly in his subconscious during sleep.

Rituals are fun and provide security.

The whole family benefits from a morning and evening ritual.

3. The positive focus

Numerous studies prove: If you focus on a child's strengths, it develops positively. If you only pay attention to your "mistakes," more and more problems arise.

We intuitively do it right for the baby - we look at everything positive and are happy about its progress every day. For hours, young parents tell what their baby can do with shining eyes. Many even write this down in a baby album or diary. Sleepless nights and shouting, on the other hand, are quickly forgotten.

Later, unfortunately, the focus is increasingly on the

weaknesses, errors, and problems of the child.

For the development and self-esteem of your child (and incidentally also for YOUR mood), it is much more helpful if you keep the positive focus and consciously concentrate on your child's strengths, successes, and moments of happiness!

Always focus on your child's strengths.

Idea: Keep a "success book" in which you record all positive experiences with your child.

4. Unconditional love

Love your child - no matter what it does!

Of course, you don't have to love everything it does. But NEVER give your child the feeling that you no longer love them. Unconditional love is the basic requirement to empower your child emotionally. In the new StarkeKids guide, I will tell you how you put your love into action so that your child can also perceive it.

This is particularly important if he behaved incorrectly, and you have to scold him. This is the only way for your child to develop positive self-esteem and healthy self-love.

Deprivation of love as punishment means that your child will later become dependent on the love of others. It will then always try to fulfill everyone else's wishes for fear of not being loved anymore. A self-determined and happy life is hardly possible.

NEVER use love deprivation as a punishment!

Unconditional love is the basis for emotional strength.

5. Sport for more confidence?

Sport is often recommended to increase self-confidence.

Basically, this is correct, but be careful! Before you register your child in a club, pay attention to the following points:

How much does performance count?

How high is the competition?

How does the trainer deal with the children if they lose?

Check this carefully and let your child take a few trial lessons first.

The weaker your child's self-confidence is, the more comfortable it will feel in a sport were participating and making an effort count more than winning.

Sport is great for your child's self-confidence, when it's fun and not under too much pressure to perform.

6. Mindfulness

Always give your child your full attention; otherwise, it will feel unimportant and not taken seriously.

A child's self-esteem develops primarily through the reactions it receives from its environment. Not paying attention means: I am not worthy of attention.

Therefore: listen to him attentively when it tells you something. Look right when it shows you something. Don't read messages on your phone when you play together...

If you don't have time for your child, explain to them. Best to promise him that it will get your undivided attention later. Then there is more to it than just being observed all day half-heartedly.

Mindfulness strengthens your child's self-esteem. Pay close attention to him.

When it tells or shows you something, it's best to go on an equal footing.

7. Endure boredom

Nowadays, children are hardly used to being boring thanks to television, the Internet, tablets and the like. If the sentence "I am so bored..." comes up, most adults immediately try to come up with some activities.

However, boredom is important for your child! On the one side, it serves as a short break from the constant flood of information of our time. On the other hand, creativity and ingenuity can only develop if your child is encouraged to do so. Therefore, try to allow and endure your child's boredom without immediately suggesting a list of ideas.

In this way, it learns to look for activities that it enjoys. It will also be more active and creative later, instead of spending his free time in front of the television or the computer.

Boredom promotes your child's creativity and ingenuity.

So let yourself get bored without immediately being distracted.

8. Allow tears

Feelings are important. This also applies to negative feelings such as anger, pain, and grief. Do not try to talk your child out of feeling ("It is not that bad ...") or to blame him ("Now pull yourself together!") Distraction is not helpful either!

All these measures mean that your child will always have problems dealing with negative feelings later. It will try to ignore them, which in the worst case, can make you sick. It will feel guilty if it has negative feelings. It will try to distract itself (with sweets, alcohol, parties, etc.)

So teach your child that negative feelings are not a bad thing. That they belong to life and want to be felt.

Killern the tears at your child; just take it in your arms, understand and wait until it calms down by itself. This also applies to boys!

If your child is unhappy or crying, just hug him or her until it calms down.

9. The bad mood is allowed

Bad moods are also allowed. After all, you're not always in a great mood, are you?

If your child feels that they shouldn't be in a bad mood, they will suppress their feelings later. It will always pretend that everything is fine while feeling bad inside. That makes you sick in the long run. Headaches, tension, stomach problems... but also depression is ultimately the result of suppressed feelings.

So allow your child to be in a bad mood. But teach him not to let his mood slip-on others. Better give him a retreat where he can "grumble" in peace (e.g., with a relaxing mental story...)

Don't expect your child to be always in a good mood.

10. Let children help

Children like to help if you let them. Small children, for example, find it totally exciting in the kitchen. Unfortunately, their enthusiasm is often slowed down because they mess everything up a bit, or you need twice as long thanks to their "help". Later you complain that your teenage boy does a big job ...

So let your child help if they want to. Even if everything takes longer, chaos arises or something breaks. It is only through experience that your child learns, builds self-confidence and skills. And so it does not lose the fun of helping with the household.

Very important:

Never blame him if something goes wrong. Imagine you are trying something new, for example, a new sport or even a new profession. Everything is taken away from you on the very first day with the words, "You can't do that yet!"

Then how are you ever supposed to learn it? And above all: how does it feel?

Not good, is it? Your child is no different...

Rejoice if your child wants to help you. This is the only way to learn something!

11. Gain experience

Your child would also like to learn in all other areas of life. It wants to develop and try new things.

Let it do as much as you can and be patient. Don't help him right away if something doesn't work right away. This is the only way to have success in the end and strengthen self-esteem. It teaches you not to give up on the first small hurdle.

Only intervene when asked to do so or offer your help in a friendly manner after a while.

Always keep in mind that something like closing the buttons is as difficult as juggling. Give your child a chance to practice and finally be incredibly proud when they have.

Let your child try out as much as possible - even if it takes longer or does not work right away. Only practice makes perfect.

12. Provide backing

Even if you want your child to have as many experiences as possible on their own, it needs the feeling that you are ALWAYS there. Being completely on your own makes you anxious and insecure.

Be observed like the driving instructor who sits next to you, answered questions on request and only intervene when things get dangerous. In this way, your child develops confidence in himself and his abilities and dares to try something new at any time.

This basic trust also strengthens your child when you are not directly with him. It is then much easier to let go (for example, when it comes to kindergarten).

Your child should always be able to rely on you and know that you can help them in an emergency.

That strengthens his confidence, and it gets braver.

13. Let your child set limits

Your child also has the right to privacy and personal limits.

The best example of this is visiting other children. For parents, it is usually a matter of course that their own children let other children play with their toys. If there is shouting in the children's room, the child is accused of being selfish and cannot share.

But honestly - do you want YOUR visitors to clear out your closets and just use whatever they like?

Discuss the situation with your child BEFORE and let them decide which toys others can and can't use. What is taboo is locked away.

Let your child define their own limits in other areas. Then help him to respect them and above all respect them yourself. Later it will be much easier for your child to say NO and to assert himself.

Your child can set clear boundaries to others.

This is how it learns that you don't have to put up with everything.

14. Accept the child's opinion

Your child must not only have its own limits, but also its own opinion.

Would you like it to stand by his opinion later, not to put up with everything and to say confidently when something doesn't suit him? Then allow your child to do that now. Do not expect blind obedience. Even if it is a bit more strenuous to discuss each point together - it is very helpful for your child's self-confidence.

However, teach him to express his opinion in a way that doesn't hurt anyone.

The advantage:

If your child learns from the start that their opinion is important and respected, there are far fewer problems during puberty. Appreciation and respect are the best prevention against rebellious teenagers.

Take your child's opinion seriously. To be respected and accepted strengthens your child's self-esteem and prevents conflicts.

15. Mistakes are great

A child cannot develop without making mistakes. An error signals to him "it doesn't work like this" or "you still have to practice that". Mistakes help to find the right solution.

For a child, mistakes are not a bad thing. Watch a child learning to walk. It tries again and again and does not give up after the first failed attempts.

Only when a child is criticized for mistakes does it become afraid of making mistakes. Anyone who is afraid becomes insecure and can no longer do anything new. Therefore NEVER criticize if your child makes mistakes! Why not ask how this (wrong) solution came about and whether it has another idea how it could work out. Don't give him the solution.

This way your child learns to deal with mistakes in a relaxed manner. It learns to trust its abilities and not to give up immediately. With this attitude, it will be much more successful later in school and at work.

Mistakes are opportunities to develop further.

Never criticize your child for making a mistake!

16. Absolute honesty

ALWAYS be honest with your child. With this you create

trust and security. Your child will be much more open, honest and authentic. At the same time, you prevent mistrust from going through life...

If you are not honest and your child experiences something else, it becomes suspicious. Then how will it know if it can rely on your words? Is it as great as you say at school, for example?

So don't tell your child, for example, that the syringe doesn't hurt at all at the doctor because it does. Be honest: "It will prick, but that can be endured and quickly forgotten afterwards."

The honest you are with your child, the more you trust it.

Avoid "little white lies" if possible.

17. Why, why, why?

Children ask 1,000 questions.

Even if it is annoying at times: take it seriously and try to answer it. This is the only way your child will become communicative and will dare to speak to other people and ask questions later. Children are only shy when they are afraid of making a fool of themselves or being stupid...

And questions are always positive: Your child is interested and wants to learn something. You should support that!

Confidence Tip: Questions

If you really have no time and no nerves to ask, explain to your child. For example, tell him: "Honey, I just have to concentrate here and so I can't answer your questions now. Can you remember them until after dinner? "

This way your child learns that it has not done anything wrong, but that it is just not the right time.

Answer your child's questions as much as possible. This strengthens his communication skills and prevents him from becoming shy.

18. Never compare

NEVER compare your child - not with siblings, not with other children and also not with yourself ("So when I was your age...") Every person is unique, with its own strengths and weaknesses. Comparing always means that you feel inferior, inferior and inadequate. This is absolutely deadly for self-confidence.

But what is great: compare your child with themselves if they develop positively! Say something like: "Look, last week you didn't dare to go on the slide alone and now it works wonderfully!"

This will strengthen your child's self-confidence and help them to be proud of their abilities.

Everyone is unique, so comparisons are pointless and very harmful to self-esteem.

19. Friendly arrangements

Treat your child the way you want to be treated. Do

not order it around like a dog and please do not ask for blind obedience. Do you want it to be pushed around by the boss or partner later?

Discuss your wishes and expectations with him and also explain why this is important to you.

Above all, let him know in good time if you want something from him and try to put yourself in the child's shoes: when a child is playing, it is fully absorbed and will not suddenly leave everything behind to sit at the lunch table a minute later. Announce something in time. You will notice that your child will then fulfill your wishes much faster and more relaxed.

Let your child know in advance if you want something from them.

Your child feels taken seriously and you avoid "theater and shouting".

20. Peaceful communication

Words can be very hurtful. Regarding children, unfortunately, we are often not aware of how harmful our statements can be for their self-esteem. Of course, we don't do this on purpose... It is all the more important to really pay attention to what you say to children.

Imagine your boss calling you an incompetent idiot who can never get anything done and is of no use at all. It doesn't feel great, does it?

Do you think that's exaggerated? Then pay attention to how people sometimes talk to children. ("You are always too late... you have to tell yourself everything three times... you are simply impossible... can you do something right?")

As a rule of thumb:

Talk to your child like a dear friend. Show respect and appreciation. Don't speak judgmental and personally hurtful. Avoid generalizations.

Even if you have to criticize your child, you can do it in an appreciative way.

Always pay attention to your words! Talk to your child like you would a friend.

21. Give proper praise

Praise is great. However, false and exaggerated praise can also make your child dependent on praise and recognition. Therefore, pay attention to when and what you praise.

For example, if your child has painted a picture for you, he wants to make you happy and not know whether he painted the picture great or not.

We tend to rate everything too much and judge it as "right or wrong" or "good or bad". This means that we are personally offended and hurt if others do not recognize our performance or our boss never says how great he thinks our work is.

Instead, encourage your child to be proud of themselves. Then it will trust its capabilities later without needing constant confirmation from others.

Praise often includes a rating. However, children do not want to be constantly evaluated. Better rejoice with him when it did something great and tell him that he can be proud of himself.

22. Correctly criticize

Criticism is basically nothing more than feedback. Your child did something that you disagree with.

The whole thing becomes problematic because you are annoyed or disappointed and then react not emotionally and calmly, but emotionally. In the worst case, you become loud and insult your child from above. With this you really lower his self-confidence.

Therefore, get in the habit of taking three deep breaths and walking eye to eye with your child before scolding him. Your voice should sound serious and strict, but it doesn't have to be louder.

The best form of criticism is NOT to criticize GAR! Instead of talking about what displeases you, say what you want.

Always try to adhere to the following pattern: state facts, talk about your feelings, external desires and also respect your child's opinion.

Here is a practical example:

Your child always throws his jacket on the floor in the hallway. Instead of complaining, you say: "Your jacket is lying on the floor here every day. (Fact) I think it looks pretty messy (your feelings). I would like you to just hang them on the hook there (wish). Or maybe you have a better suggestion? " (Appreciation)

Criticize as calmly as possible and according to the following pattern: State facts, talk about your feelings, say what you want and also listen to your child's opinion.

23. Be a role model

The most important thing is to be a role model for your child.

Children imitate us, watch us and hear more than we think. They feel exactly when you yourself are anxious or insecure. That is why everything that strengthens YOUR self-confidence is also helpful for your child.

The best tips and exercises to acquire a strong and healthy self-confidence can be found here: Strengthening self-confidence

Strong parents have strong children!

Everything that is good for your self-confidence is therefore also good for your child.

Summary: This is how you strengthen your child's self-confidence with ease

Now you have got a lot of tips with which you can build and support your child's self-confidence.

Basically, it's very simple:

Treat your child the way you want to be treated!

Do you want to be ordered around, ignored, patronized, ridiculed, teased, punished?

Do you always want to be nice and smile no matter how you're doing?

Do you want to be afraid of making mistakes and always have to be perfect?

Do you want to put up with everything just to be "good"?

Do you always want to do what others expect or ask of you, even if you don't feel like doing it at all?

Always ask yourself how you would feel right now instead of your child. It will be all the easier for you to educate yourself to be a strong, lovable and confident personality.

FREQUENTLY ASKED QUESTIONS ON THE TOPIC OF "STRENGTHENING SELF-CONFIDENCE IN CHILDREN"

Do Bach flowers, globules and Co. help make my child more confident?

A low self-esteem in children can also be positively influenced by homeopathic remedies or Bach flowers.

However, you must not expect miracles from it. The effect of these funds is primarily based on strengthening the existing potential that lies dormant in your child. If you give him globules or drops and tell him at the same time that these "magic balls" or "mother drops" will make him strong and brave, you will definitely achieve clear results. The effect of homeopathic remedies is then positively supported by the power of "mental suggestion".

Our mental stories work on the same principle. Thanks to the special storytelling method, regular listening has been proven to make your child calmer, braver and more confident.

Conclusion: blue flowers and homeopathy can be a valuable support for your child. With our mental stories you can significantly increase the effect, since they directly "program" your child's subconscious.

Are there books or CDs that strengthen my child's self-confidence?

There are stories - whether in the form of books, audiobooks or films - that can strengthen your child's self-confidence. It is imperative that only positive messages are conveyed in the story and that your child can identify with the main character.

Most of the time, however, it unfortunately looks like this: The stories are about brave heroes or heroines who experience all kinds of adventures and bravely survive all dangers. Your child only experiences these adventures as a "spectator". In the worst case, it starts to compare itself to the main character. If he then feels much less brave, strong and brave, his self-esteem even suffers as a result.

Our mental stories are therefore specially written so that when you listen to them, your child becomes a hero yourself and then has the feeling that you have experienced and mastered the adventure yourself. Even if these success stories only take place in his imagination, they are imprinted on your child's subconscious as well as real experiences. Over time, it becomes increasingly courageous and confident.

Are there different phases in which my child is more or less confident?

Yes, in any case!

Each child goes through several phases in its development, in which ups and downs alternate. Your brave and confident child can suddenly become anxious and insecure from one day to the next, even if there has been no particular incident that would explain this change.

The most important thing is that you then understand your child. Statements like "What's wrong with YOU all at once?" Or "Now you didn't do it that way, you've done it 100 times." Are completely out of place. Your child is already insecure enough.

It is currently on the way to a new development stage and needs your full support.

Imagine that you were promoted: Although you still have the same colleagues around you and are sitting in the same office, everything is suddenly new and unfamiliar. You just need a while to get used to the new situation.

In such phases of development, it is particularly important that you follow the tips mentioned above. The advantage is that your child is particularly receptive to positive and strengthening messages during this time! Use this opportunity. (e.g. through the increased use of mental stories...)

What influence do teachers, educators and peers have on my child?

The older your child is, the more influence other people have on their development. Many parents are afraid that their child's self-esteem will be destroyed by other people's negative behavior.

In particular, peers and older children can put your child's self-confidence to the test. But even teachers and educators do not always behave as it would be helpful for your child.

But these experiences are important! Your child will always meet people in his life against whom he must assert himself. It can only learn this by practicing to deal with such people. It is a training program, so to speak, that makes your child stronger.

(If it does suffer from bullying, then you should definitely help him. Here you can find all the information: My child is being bullied - 12 strategies against bullying at school)

The self-esteem that YOU give your child is the most

important prerequisite for mastering such "tests". The more support, security and trust you give your child, the easier it is to cope with external influences. And it's never too late to empower your child in this regard!

KID ABUSE TYPES

1. *Physical abuse*

Physical abuse is caused by physical injury to the child. In general, it can be understood that the child who is hurt from the parent can be called for medical help late and the number of old wounds. Recurrence rate of physical abuse is 20%.

2. *Sexual abuse*

Sexual abuse of children. Suicide attempts, escaping from school and asocial behavior disorders are the most important symptoms. Child sexual abuse is most commonly seen between 6-10 years of age. The rate of girls in abuse is higher than the rate of boys.

3. *Emotional abuse*

Psychological verbal abuse of the child. Scolding, insulting, scorning, threatening, accusing, resenting the child, pretending not to exist, mocking the child are some of the emotional abuse. One of the types of abuse may be single or multiple may exist in the same child. In particular, emotional abuse is almost always associated with other types of abuse.

Excessive aggression in children's behavior, from extreme aggression to passivity as a result of emotional abuse exhibits. The child shows delayed physical, emotional or intellectual development.

4.   *Intentionally damaging*

Typically, mothers are responsible. A deliberate harm to a child by a mother or father. They usually receive medical attention after this behavior.

RISK FACTORS FOR KIDS ABUSE

Considering the factors posing the risk of abuse according to the ecological model, the following factors come to the fore.

It is known that children who were born prematurely and who have been hospitalized for a long time during the treatment period are exposed to more abuse. In such cases, emotional ties-trust ties do not occur between the mother and the child, since bilateral breastfeeding is not performed in the critical period. There may be situations where the mother rejects the child and disrupts her care. Therefore, especially in cases of physical abuse, premature birth and absence of mother-child bond is one of the most important risk factors.

Social and institutional factors

- High crime rate

- Absence or scarcity of social services

- High poverty rate

- High unemployment rate

Family-related factors

- Physical or sexual abuse in childhood

- Parents get married at a young age

- Single parent

- Stepfather

- Emotional insufficiency

- Poor communication ability

- Lack of self-esteem

- Alcohol-drug addicted parent

- Lack of social support

- Domestic violence

- Family with many children

- Mental illness in the family

- Unwanted pregnancy

- Adopted child

Child-related factors

- Premature birth or low birth weight

- Physically or mentally handicapped child

- Hyperactive or grumpy child

- Infants who are separated from the mother for a long time after birth for various reasons

- Prevent child abuse

Reasons

- Conflict, unhappy marriage and verbal violence in the child's family.

- Stepmother or father.

- Lack of equal distribution of decision-making in the family.

- Problems that arise around the economic and sudden changes experienced by the family.

- Families remain indifferent to social organizations.

- Traditional family structure and physical punishment.

Prevention Methods

The method of preventing child abuse can be grouped under three main headings:

1. The first method is to provide a wide range of public education. Such activities are aimed at changing families that will abuse and neglect their children in the future. At this level, there are public education activities, family education classes and family support programs in the community. The impact of these first-level studies is uncertain, as they are intended to prevent them before they exist.

2. The second method is aimed at families who have previously abused and neglected their children, young families, families with children in need of

care, individuals with children (without mother or father) and low-income families. The second method foresees that family and child education should be given to high-risk families and ignores their children being disabled or stepchildren.

3. The third method is for families that have been formally identified and who are constantly abusing violence and neglect against their children. It was foreseen that these families would be prevented in accordance with the laws and courts.

WHY DON'T CHILDREN TALK ABOUT WHAT THEY'RE GOING THROUGH?

- They may feel unbelievable.

- They may fear they're in trouble.

- They may be afraid of the threat of the abuser.

- They may want to protect the abuser, they may love the abuser, but they don't like what they do.

- They may not know how to tell.

- They may not know that sexual violence is wrong.

- They may be afraid of being ostracized by friends.

- They may be ashamed of discussing sexual matters with their elders.

- They may not want to be called sneakers.

- how to name and explain it, foolish.

- As they do not try to prevent what is done to them,

they may feel guilty and become They may have been told that good children should not use sexual words.

- They may not be able to comprehend what has been done because of their ignorance about sexuality and / or sexual harassment / abuse, they cannot know silent.

- They may believe that they should have absolute trust and obedience to the abuser because of his age and / or his position of power in the family.

- Because they are children, they may not think that it is natural for them to wonder about sexual abuse, to try to learn by play, that this does not mean that they themselves are guilty.

- If they have been sexually stimulated and enjoyment during the abuse, they may believe that the exploiter's actions are voluntary.

- He spoke of a period and blamed themselves, excluded, refusing to empathize with the child from the perspective of the abuser, condescending, humiliating, pitiful, and so on. They may face reactions, they may endure their fear of telling false reactions.

- They may be afraid of being abused again by the people they tell about sexual abuse.

- If they are locked at the moment of sexual abuse and have closed themselves to external-internal reactions, they can be prevented by experiencing an same reaction when trying to speak of abuse.

- Even if they have enough information about violence, sexual violence and sexuality, they may be afraid to call their experiences as sexual abuse;

- They may be hiding because they are ashamed of the degrading, suppressive nature of the action taken.

CONCLUSION

Why self-confidence is so important for your child

A strong self-confidence is the best prerequisite for a happy and successful life. Confident children get along much better in life.

Confident children...

- are more successful - if you know your strengths and don't let your weaknesses slow you down, it will be much easier at school and later at work

- have more friends - those who dare to approach others openly and courageously will find friends much easier

- are healthier - those who feel valuable, respected and useful are much less susceptible to depression, burnout and psychosomatic illnesses

- resist temptations - those who are strong enough (and can, for example, defend themselves against group pressure) are not easily tempted to smoke or take drugs

- have fewer fears - those who believe in themselves and know that they can master small defeats are more courageous and can do a lot more

- are more creative - those who like to try new things and are not deterred by challenges can gain a lot more experience and develop their talents

- Live safer - inner strength already signals through body language that a child does not put up with everything. This is an important protection against bullying, violence and abuse!

- later have happy relationships - those who feel loved and do not constantly doubt themselves, appear more positive and attractive to other people and thus have more harmonious relationships

- go their own way - those who are confident in their own wishes and goals are not so easily influenced and pushed around by others